THAT
TERRIBLE
WOMAN

First published 2024

COPYRIGHT © JACKI RACKE 2024

The moral right of Jacki Racke to be authorised
as the author of this work has been asserted by her.

No part of this book may be reproduced or transmitted by any means, except as permitted by UK copyright law or the author. For licensing requests, please contact the author at jackiracke@gmail.com

Paperback: 978-1-0686253-0-5

Hardback: 978-1-0686253-1-2

Kindle: 978-1-0686253-2-9

Book Design by DAMONZA

I dedicate this book to my beloved parents, Irene and Monty, and to the love of my life, my husband, Laurance.

To my treasured daughters Emma and Kelly, my adored grandchildren, Charlie, Georgina, Ella, Jack, Joshua, Tazmin, Jessica and Sophie and to Trevor and Juliet, my much-loved stepchildren, all of whom bring me so much joy.

Author's Note

This is a work of fiction. Unless otherwise indicated, all the names, characters, businesses, places, events and incidents in this book are either the product of the author's imagination or used in a fictitious manner, and all conversations are imagined. Any resemblance to actual persons, living or dead, or actual events, is purely coincidental.

THAT TERRIBLE WOMAN

JACKI RACKE

You can live your life to avenge your past or enrich your future

Edith Eger

CHAPTER ONE

Tuesday

IT WAS TWENTY years to the day since Don had choked on a chicken bone and had the audacity to leave Edna all alone.

Standing in her bathroom, the walls of which were a hideous shade of salmon pink, she vigorously brushed her teeth and saw a strange old lady scowling back at her. Baggy eyes, turkey neck, grey hair grown coarse and wild. She studied the face and mused about what had happened so that she now cared so little about her appearance.

What indeed!

She was distracted, thinking about how she would celebrate the memory of Don's passing this year. Announcing to the empty room as if her beloved Don was still there:

'I think I'll start with a fry-up with runny eggs, perfectly browned tomatoes and super moist mushrooms. Two slices of sourdough toast and lashings of butter and apricot jam, just like you always liked, my dear.' Edna was almost drooling at the thought. 'After that we should go to Frimlington Woods; the bluebells should be out now. That was one of our favourite walks, wasn't it? Then let's…'

Edna suddenly became aware that her telephone was ringing.

She made her way into the bedroom, irritated that the caller was intruding on her thoughts. She half-expected whomever it was to have hung up before she got to the phone, but no, it kept on ringing, refusing to be ignored. 'Well, whoever you are, you're really persistent. I'll give you that.' Then, thinking of her two daughters, she muttered angrily, 'What do those girls want now?'

'4742,' she enunciated clearly.

'Hello, Edna, it's Felicity,' the whiny voice declared. 'Sorry to tell you that my daddy passed away last night.'

Silence. Edna couldn't stand her cousin, Felicity, who represented everything that irritated her and far more. Even stronger was her dislike, in fact, her hatred for Felicity's father, who was Edna's Uncle Harold, and she couldn't stand his wife, Betty, either. They were the people Edna held responsible for all the insecurities and unhappiness that had dogged her throughout her life.

When they were children, Edna was always expected to play second fiddle to Felicity, her younger cousin by only nine months. She was never allowed to have her own way, and the list of her complaints was long. Edna resented the fact that she never got to decide anything. It was always: 'Let Felicity choose, she's only little! Let Felicity have the bus ticket, the last sweet, the choice of TV programme,' and a host of other things that Edna felt were grossly unfair. If there was one chocolate left in the box, it was given to Felicity. She repeatedly complained to her mother, Iris, about why everything had to be what Felicity wanted. When Edna passed her eleven-plus there was weak applause, yet if Felicity came first in the egg and spoon race it was cause for a great celebration party. To compound it, Felicity was their paternal grandmother's favourite. When she and Edna's grandfather arrived home from a holiday trip her grandmother would hand Felicity a package. Edna would stand biting her lip, watching her cousin excitedly ripping open the beautifully wrapped gift containing a doll, a dress, or suchlike, whilst

Edna could only stare with disappointment and, yes, resentment. The horrid woman would then turn to Edna and say, 'Sorry, Edna, they just didn't have anything for a little girl of your age!'

No one ever pointed out that they were almost identical in age. What could possibly have been construed as inappropriate for a child only nine months older? At other times, her grandmother would come back from a trip and say, 'There was nothing for Felicity, so I could hardly buy for you and not for her, could I, Edna?'

Why not? Edna wanted to scream. She hated playing poor relation to Felicity, the wonder child. It was hardly Felicity's fault, but over the years, Edna had built up an inexplicable resentment toward the poor girl. This call was stirring up all kinds of unpleasant feelings. She especially didn't want to think about 'the incident' that had occurred when she was only five years old and which had haunted her ever since. Sadly, any action, like an innocent call from her cousin, managed to bring it immediately to mind, drawing it quite firmly into the headlights again.

'Hello, Edna, are you there? Did you hear me?'

'Yes, I heard you. Harold is dead, and you will let me know about the funeral arrangements. I think that's about it, isn't it?'

'I thought...' Edna could hear the woman clearing her throat nervously as she tried again. 'Oh, never mind. I will send you the arrangements as soon as the funeral has been organised.'

Felicity sounded close to tears. Edna knew that her cousin couldn't have any idea why she disliked her so much because Harold and Betty had insisted on protecting Felicity, not wanting to frighten her. In fact, the incident had long since been forgotten by everyone. That is, everyone but Edna. She desperately wanted to tell the pathetic woman, whose demeanour was always as pitiful as her appearance, that she had no intention of attending her ghastly father's funeral but decided not to. After all, none of it was Felicity's fault, so best not to be rude. As difficult as Edna could be, she was nothing if not fair.

'Well, thank you, Felicity, for the update on your father's demise. As you know, your parents and I were not close, but I do thank you for bringing it to my attention.' *Oh dear, even for me that was harsh!*

Without giving her stunned cousin a chance to respond, Edna mumbled a weak apology, excusing herself to answer a non-existent caller at the front door.

She was angry with Felicity for disturbing her because the mere sound of Felicity's voice had the power to drag up the horrific details of that fateful day. That moment in time invaded her thoughts and just would not let go.

Feeling ravenous, Edna made her way gingerly down the stairs. Whenever Edna was anxious, two things happened. Her enormous appetite intensified, and so would the need to take a therapeutic bath in order to calm her nerves. She wandered into her once-glossy Wrighton kitchen with Hotpoint stove and Electrolux fridge, all of which had definitely seen better days. She opened the tap and poured water into her whistling kettle. Other than the Americans, most people in the UK had thrown them out years ago, but Edna couldn't see the point in spending money on a new-fangled electric one when hers worked perfectly well. Now in a really bad mood, she reluctantly abandoned the idea of the fry-up to honour her husband's passing and poured a generous portion of bran into a Denby bowl, not noticing that the paint around the rim was worn and the colour more a dirty grey now than the original cornflower blue. She sliced a banana on top of the crisp flakes, sprinkled brown sugar liberally over the top, and finished off with a copious amount of whole milk, which was delivered daily by Bert, the local 'milkie'. She detested supermarket cartons; in fact, she abhorred all of today's modern packaging, preferring to go back to her childhood of brown paper bags and glass bottles. Now that there was a worldwide attempt to protect the environment, Edna was more than slightly smug about her long-held attitude.

Slowly, a thought began to dawn on her. *I wonder if I shouldn't just take the opportunity of the old man's death to wreak my revenge. I shall go to the funeral, if only to tell that horrid wife of his what she and her husband did to me. I will shame her into admitting what they did.*

She hesitated, her resolve weakening.

'What do you think, Don?' she asked of the empty room. After all these years, it never failed to upset her that there was no response.

Small-boned and just over five foot tall, but weighing in at around 140 pounds due to her overblown stomach, she appeared much bigger than she actually was. Having smoked sixty cigarettes a day from the age of fifteen, she had a very throaty voice, and people were generally disappointed when they met the person associated with the sexy voice on the end of the telephone. Rude to neighbours and delivery people with her barbed tongue, she wasn't popular and, in fact, was quite often disliked. With age and life's knocks, Edna believed that she had earned the right to be dry and sarcastic and would often articulate what many people thought but were not brave enough to say out loud. She could be very intolerant, particularly struggling to hide her frustration and immense irritation at people she saw as stupid.

She had a sour face and ate with her mouth open. The milk from her cereal dripped down her chin in a most undignified way. Her manners were incongruous for a woman so well-spoken, a reflection of the privileged life that she had once enjoyed. Every now and then, she wiped the milk carelessly away with the back of her hand, rubbing it on her flannelette dressing gown. The gown bore the faint scent of Estee Lauder Youth Dew, a throwback from her childhood. With one whiff, in an instant she was a little girl again, sitting on Hampstead Heath with a whole world in front of her…

As she sat at the breakfast table rubbing her arthritic legs, she wondered when her knees had become ninety years old, and where it had all gone wrong.

Her mind wandered back to her father's mother, and how Edna used to wish that the horrid woman would go away and leave them alone, but then the object of her resentment suddenly died, and Edna cried for weeks, causing confusion for everyone, with her refusing to divulge the source of her sadness.

Edna remembered how her mother had tried, without success, to get at the truth; to understand why Edna was affected so badly by her grandmother's death.

'Edna, darling, why are you sad?' Iris had asked her. 'I didn't realise that you were so attached to your grandmother. Tell us, please. What's the matter?' Iris and Richard, her father, had tried and tried to get her to talk, but the sad little girl would say nothing. Then finally, one day:

'I killed her,' Edna cried, the anguish and shame spilling in a torrent of tears.

'What? Edna, why on earth would you think that?'

'Because I wanted her to go away,' she wailed. 'It's all my fault and I'm a bad person.'

'Listen, my angel. You are *not* a bad person. You are a lovely, adorable, sweet, and kind little girl. You cannot wish anyone dead. It's just not possible. You can't make me Queen just because you wish it for me. Likewise, you can't cause me to win the Premium Bonds tomorrow. Life just doesn't work that way. You can want and hope all you like, but things like that are beyond our control and happen because they are part of life's grand plan. Nothing any of us say or do will change that. Your grandmother died because it was her time to go and not because of anything that you wished or said.'

Edna remembered sitting there watching her beautiful mother with her ash blonde hair and large blue eyes. She was just full of wonder and love that Iris, her amazing mummy, always had the ability to make things better.

'Could you make me a cheese and tomato sauce sandwich, please, Mummy?' Edna had found her appetite again, and although this strange concoction was normally reserved for Richard to make when he was left in sole charge, today she didn't care who made it. She was a complete mix of happy and hungry.

The silence in the house was suddenly disturbed by yet another flipping telephone call bringing Edna back to the present. Apart from her bi-weekly calls from her two daughters, Olivia and Viola, Edna hardly ever received phone calls these days, yet this morning she was being plagued with them. She hobbled out into the hall.

'Yes?' Edna barked rudely down the phone. She didn't even bother to say '4742' this time.

'Good morning, Mrs Watson. Allow me to introduce myself. My name is Edward Clitheroe. My wife and I have admired your house with its gorgeous gardens for many years and would like to talk to you about it. I wonder if I could make an appointment to come and see you.'

'How do you know my name, and where did you get my number from?' Edna was irritated but, at the same time, intrigued.

'I looked you up on the internet,' he bumbled.

'The internet! What could the internet possibly know about my personal information, and what is it that you actually want to discuss, other than perhaps admiring my roses?'

'I want to talk to you about the possibility of making you a handsome offer to buy your house.'

Not bloody likely! she mumbled under her breath. Edna was just about to refuse when her insatiable curiosity got the better of her. There was that strange note left outside her door yesterday morning: DON'T LOOK A GIFT HORSE IN THE MOUTH! GRAB OPPORTUNITIES WITH BOTH HANDS. She had found it inside her *Daily Mail*, and, whilst she had dismissed it as complete nonsense, something had made her keep it. She had placed it inside the dresser drawer and had completely forgotten about it until now.

'You can come at eleven o'clock tomorrow. Not a moment earlier, as I have my routine, which must not be disturbed.'

'Yes, of course, I will be there at eleven on the dot. Should you wish to contact me my number is….' But before he could utter another word, the line had gone dead. As far as Edna was concerned, the conversation was most definitely over.

❦

Shocked at Edna's rudeness, Edward called his boss, Reg Hopkins, at Trident Property Developers.

'Mission accomplished. I tell you, Reg, it worked, and it was much easier than I thought. She's agreed to see me at eleven tomorrow morning. Honestly Reg, I can hardly believe my luck.'

'I hope you didn't say where you were from?' the gruff voice snarled down the phone.

'No, of course not. In fact, surprisingly, she didn't ask anything at all other than wanting to know how I got her number and insisting that I wasn't to be late. Sounded like a right old battle axe, but don't worry, she'll never be able to resist my incomparable charm.'

'Your charm is debatable, Edward, and not something I care to dwell upon,' Reg retaliated. 'Just remember that the whole deal depends upon you getting us her house. This is the one that we are going to retire on, Edward, so don't screw up.'

In fact, Edward was not a good negotiator. He was an expert bookkeeper but had no commercial acumen. His boss, however, was so lazy that he would rather delegate to an unskilled Edward than do the job proficiently himself. No, Reg Hopkins came from a school that believed that his job was to sit and bark orders without ever dirtying his own hands!

Edna had no idea that adjoining her back garden of just under an acre was a site that Trident had purchased with a view to building two blocks of flats and twelve townhouses. Nor did she know that her house was the only thing standing in the way of Trident gaining planning permission.

Edward knew that everything hinged on getting Edna Watson to sell to Trident. Oh yes, he was supremely aware that if he wanted to keep his job, he had to get it right.

Still smarting from the disturbances of the morning, Edna wanted to enjoy one more mug of tea. Try as she could, she just couldn't relax. Something strange was going on, but what?

Normally she bathed in the morning, this being her time to reflect and remember, but today, having been delayed by the call, it wasn't possible. She abandoned her tea and went up to her bedroom, opened the wardrobe, being careful to avert her eyes away from the top shelf. She dressed quickly in her fleecy tracksuit and then made her way downstairs to organise supper before leaving. She re-entered the kitchen and peered into the fridge. Edna still missed Don terribly, and never more so than today. Looking for inspiration as to what to make for supper, she chatted to him. 'So, what do you think of the Taylor's extension? I think it's vulgar and not in keeping with our village at all! So what would you like for our special dinner tonight, love? Shall we have lamb chops? Good, we've some fresh mint in the garden, so I'll pop that in with the new potatoes. Come on, love. Let's get going for our walk.'

Edna loved lamb chops so much that it was one of the few meals for which she actually made a real effort, because other meals were too much of a faff to clear up on a regular basis. Dressed in her grey anorak and walking boots, she grabbed her walking stick before locking the door carefully behind her. In no time she was walking through Frimlington Woods, which had always been that special and safe place for her and Don. The violet glow of the bluebells, the jewel in the crown of Spring, dazzled her senses. Delving into her pocket she pulled out a toffee and popped it into her mouth. Suddenly everything seemed calmer. 'Ooh, Don, isn't this just perfect?' she announced. Chattering away to Don as if he were with her, she strolled for almost two hours, indulging in all the delights that Spring had to offer.

Feeling like she could eat a horse, she stopped at her favourite café and strode in. It was hard to choose what she wanted to order these days because they made such strange concoctions like smashed avocado, whatever that was, or buffalo mozzarella and tomato, which Edna found completely tasteless. *What about a good old egg and tomato or roast beef and horseradish?* Not one for pleasantries, she barked at the poor girl, 'I'll have a cheese and pickle bap, and make it quick. I'm in a hurry.'

Edna could see that the pretty young girl was slightly taken aback upon hearing her gravelly voice, and her discomfiture amused Edna. Watching in irritation as the young woman selected a bap and proceeded to butter it slowly, Edna snapped, 'Just get on with it, will you? I don't have all day.'

'That will be three-fifty, please.' With her smile gone, the girl handed Edna the bag, and Edna wasn't even embarrassed to see the relief in the girl's face to be rid of her at last.

Edna handed the girl a five-pound note, shoved the change into her pocket, leaving no tip, and hurriedly made her way out of the shop, bashing into a woman who also had a walking stick.

'Do look where you're going, you nearly knocked me over,' Edna said rudely, and without a second glance headed off down the road. Her stomach was growling and once home, she didn't even put her bap on a plate, but chose to eat it straight out of the bag.

The call from her cousin and that Clitheroe man were both really playing on her mind. More than a little tired, not to mention still hungry, she collected the newspaper, made herself a mug of tea and carried it upstairs to her bedroom with a couple of bourbon biscuits tucked in behind her napkin for an afternoon snack. She set her alarm for three o'clock and scoffed the biscuits, planning to allow herself the luxury of an hour's rest on the bed. Edna was startled when the alarm rang, bringing her back to the present. Quickly getting off the bed, she made her way downstairs so that she could enjoy another cup of tea in the sitting room whilst watching TV.

'Oh, goodie,' she declared to a non-existent Don. 'Just in time for *Countdown*. I'm sorry about the disturbances, my love, but I'll make it up to you.'

She never read or watched TV whilst eating, except for maybe the odd biscuit. It was one of her few 'almost' disciplines. Today, that rule would be totally broken as she helped herself to two custard creams, having completely forgotten about the bourbons she had already eaten upstairs.

Edna sat there munching while shouting merciless abuse at the unhearing contestants on the screen. The programme finished and Edna congratulated herself for doing better than, or at least as well as, the contestants. Picking up the newspaper she soon nodded off, spectacles in hand, her head reclining most uncomfortably to the side, her face taking on an anxious and troubled look.

She woke with a painful crick in her neck. She massaged her neck with the Arnica balm that she kept in the top cupboard above the coffee and winced at the pain, but also at the roughness of her hands. Despite having a pot of hand cream that sat by the side of the bed, a frivolous gift from her younger daughter, Viola, she hardly ever remembered to apply it.

It was nearly time to eat again, Edna decided, her routine being seven o'clock supper, clear up and then watch another one of her favourite programmes. She had no interest in the soaps and wondered how a particular series full of ghastly common people, which had run for over thirty-five years, could hold an audience captive with just doom and gloom in every episode. *Isn't there enough unhappiness in the world?* No, Edna's taste was more for documentaries. *Panorama*, David Attenborough's *Planet Earth* and some with entertainment value, like Joanna Lumley travelling around the world or Stanley Tucci exploring food in Italy. Knowing that she would need to take a hot bath with Epsom salts after supper to ease her pain, Edna decided to leave the lamb chops for tomorrow. She selected a can with the familiar Heinz logo, full of their marvellous recipe of haricot beans in tomato sauce, which she poured into a small saucepan to heat slowly. She always placed a knob of butter in the pan, a trick that Don had taught her. Then she placed two slices of bread in the ancient toaster (another of her relics) and, hey presto, she had a scrumptious supper of baked beans on toast. Tonight, easy to prepare and wash up, was definitely the order of the day.

As well as relieving her pain, Edna hoped that the bath might help to relax her anxiety over the old memories that the call had stirred up. No one could imagine that Edna was actually insecure and vulnerable, as opposed to the outwardly strong and difficult woman that most people knew. And that was exactly how she wanted it.

She entered her dated bathroom, a complete original inherited from the previous owners, complete with black and white linoleum floor. There was a basic white bathroom suite comprising a pedestal basin, lavatory and bath with shower above. The bath was dressed with a shower curtain, being the only thing that got regularly changed because of the mould that developed from time to time. Edna leaned over the bath, opened the faucet and ran the hot water until steam enveloped the room. She carefully poured a few drops of Estee Lauder Youth Dew into the bath and watched the milky oil float on top of the water. She wiped the mirror so that it didn't obscure her image, and as she removed her Triumph bra and Sloggi panties, she stared at her rather ample bosom that always managed to stretch her T-shirts most unflatteringly across the folds of lardy flesh, revealing the damage done by twenty years of Big Macs, chips, doughnuts and a host of other unsuitable meal substitutes. With no Don to cook for, she rarely took the time to cook anything healthy for herself.

Easing into the piping hot bath, as Edna loathed anything luke-warm, including people, she lay back, closed her eyes, and inhaled the aroma. Her mother had always placed a few drops of the spicy and intoxicating blend into her bathwater, a ritual that Edna had happily continued, as it helped her not only to relax but also to feel close to her mother.

She was still upset by her cousin's call. Going to the funeral would involve her coming face to face with her aunt and stirring everything up again. Was that what she wanted? As much as she dreaded a pos-sible confrontation with that terrible woman, she was wise enough to realise that the opportunity afforded her by the funeral was what she had been waiting for her whole life. After so many years of trying to find a way to repay her aunt and uncle for the damage that they had done, this could be it. The chance to make her aunt pay, really did seem too good to miss.

Tonight, the bath didn't relax her at all, as she kept going back-wards and forwards in her head as to whether she would or would not attend the funeral. A chance to finally draw a line under the whole ugly episode, but she had to concede that this was all having a bad effect on her state of mind. The thought that this could finally settle the score literally made her shiver. Then the doubts crept in again. *Will I be able to say it, go through with it?* Edna was battling with her inner self.

'*Go for it, Edna, this is your last chance,*' her alter ego whispered in her ear. What she just couldn't decide was whether attending would provide the panacea she was looking for or just make everything worse.

As much as she normally tried not to think about it, today, prompted by the call, she found 'the incident' was very much at the forefront of her mind, as the heady scent finally lulled her into an almost semi-conscious state.

She was five years old, and her Aunt Betty and Uncle Harold had taken her to Regent's Park Zoo with her cousin Felicity. Innocent as the outing sounded, an ill-conceived attempt at a joke instigated by her aunt and uncle turned out to be one of the most profound and distressing experiences that would still plague her at the age of sixty-nine, with separation issues, a lack of self-confidence, and an inability to accept acts of kindness.

Whilst Edna lay there, recoiling at the memory of that horrific day, she began to accept that the impending funeral would indeed offer the opportunity to finally wreak revenge for what had happened to her all those years ago. An action that had ended with such disastrous consequences. Yes, she mused, attending the funeral might finally give her the chance to tell her aunt how it had damaged her. Disquieted, also, by the most perturbing call from that man called Edward Clitheroe and the strange note left on her doorstep, she found that her normally soothing bath did nothing today to quieten her thoughts.

She stepped out of the bath carefully, wrapped herself in one of her well-worn and slightly hard bath sheets, sat on her bedroom stool, inherited from her mother and far too ornate for her own bedroom, and dried herself.

She selected a nightie from the dresser drawer, brushed her hair and then felt the all too familiar rumbles in her stomach.

Despite the dentist always telling her that she ate far too much sugar, she went downstairs and made herself a cup of cocoa.

Well, it will help me sleep, she reasoned. She boiled the milk and scattered one heaped teaspoon of cocoa into the cup, watching the bits of chocolate swirl around. She then looked behind her as if someone was watching and hastily added another spoonful of the delicious powder to the mug. Holding it firmly by the handle, taking care that she did not burn herself, she took it upstairs and, sitting in the warmth of her bed, she savoured her nightcap.

Edna realised she was again looking up towards the top of her wardrobe where a canvas box lay hidden from prying eyes. As she often did, she wondered what secrets lay within that box. The box that Edna had never found the courage to open in over twenty years. All that remained of her mother lay in that box, and she had never been entirely sure why, but something in that box scared her. Scared her enough to leave it untouched for all those years.

Then, too tired to get out of bed to brush her teeth, let alone summon the courage to open the box, she turned out the light. Within moments Edna was asleep, thrashing about, throwing the bedclothes off, her body as if on fire as one of her recurring dreams took hold.

She was running as fast as her little legs would carry her, but at each turn there was a grotesque toothless gargoyle laughing at her, leaving her no room to escape. Her heart was pounding, and her cheeks were wet.

Edna sat bolt upright in bed and, despite the heart pills that she took for her Atrial Fibrillation, she felt like her heart was going to burst out of her ribcage. Her nightie was soaking, and she was dismayed to find that she was, in fact, crying real tears. She freshened herself up, pulled a clean nightie from the dresser drawer, got back into bed and finally fell asleep. It didn't occur to Edna that it might not necessarily have been the nightmare that had caused her nightie to be drenched with perspiration.

CHAPTER TWO

Wednesday

EDNA HAD SET her alarm for an hour earlier than usual so that she could enjoy her breakfast of croissant laden with lashings of butter and jam, accompanied by a nice mug of what she liked to describe as 'builder's tea' before her meeting with the man named Edward Clitheroe. She also wanted enough time to luxuriate in the bath.

She went upstairs to the bathroom, turned on the faucet and watched her elixir ebbing and flowing in the water. Hoping that the bath would soothe and comfort her, today she found it was doing anything but. She lay there longing for the scent of the Youth Dew to work it's magic. Disappointed that it was not working, she gave herself a perfunctory wash and exited the bath quickly.

She dried herself carefully, removed her underwear from the chest of drawers, and then moved to the wardrobe, selecting a pair of navy trousers and a grey twinset that in truth was too tight for her now, but then nothing really fitted well anymore. Even so, she was definitely not going to spend money on new clothes.

Yet again her eyes were drawn to the top of the wardrobe, which beckoned her to enter its web of secrets.

She reached to the top shelf, running her fingers over the rough canvas whilst wrestling with herself as to whether today was the day to open the secret box.

Still rattled by yesterday's call, which had dragged her thoughts back to the past, she was even more curious about what lay within.

She had originally found the box after her mother's untimely death at the age of sixty-one. Whilst sorting through her meagre belongings, placing the clothes into piles and deciding to which charities they should be donated, she had felt something rigid, and slowly, like discovering a spider in the bed sheets and nervous to disturb it, she had revealed a yellowed and dog-eared book. There, hidden carefully, lay the possible answers to so many questions that Edna had about her mother and, in particular, her mother's state of health. Gently caressing the worn leather, she had hesitated, so nervous to open it. She had sat there for hours wondering what to do and finally decided that she was not yet ready to deal with it. So it had lain there all these years, Edna never having found the strength to open it. She was scared that it held the answer to why her mother had died, taking her own life without warning. She was even more terrified that she would be exposing some old secrets of which she knew nothing – the fear of opening Pandora's box – after which she knew for sure that there would be no going back. Aware of the dark secret that she herself was hiding, she recognised that her mother could also have been hiding something. But what?

Edna slammed the wardrobe door shut just in time to answer the doorbell, bang on the dot of eleven o'clock. She gave the jumped-up young man (or so she thought) a piercing once over. He greeted her with a sickly smile, revealing yellowed teeth, and proffered his hand, which Edna ignored as she ushered him into the sitting room. She ordered him to sit on the lumpiest chair, not wanting him to be too comfortable. Like a trainer appraising a new mare, she continued to study him. He was tall and gangly with a pockmarked face. *Clearly he picks at his acne! Revolting creature*! She couldn't see her face in his shoes and no one had told him that a true gentleman would never wear loafers with a suit, and most definitely not brown ones. She noted that his tie was very loud and his hair too long. Poor Edward Clitheroe was failing Edna's test miserably, and it was clear that he felt most uncomfortable under her *National Geographic*-worthy microscopic eyes.

'So, young man, tell me what's so important that you need to speak to me about my house? You don't look like a gardener, nor a window cleaner, and in any case, how did you say you got my telephone number?'

Edna quite enjoyed seeing the ghastly man's obvious discomfort as she listened to him nervously clear his throat. As he spoke, she noted that he had avoided telling her how he had got her contact details.

'I've always admired your house, and my wife and I have dreamed of the possibility of living here someday.'

'And how do you propose that little scenario would come about? You, young man, are completely delusional!'

'I was wondering if there was a figure that we could offer you to tempt you to move. There must be a figure that you would accept for it. I'm prepared to offer you a handsome amount.' Edna pulled herself up to her most formidable stance and was pleased to see that he looked even more uncomfortable as she remained silent. She continued to stare at him with her steely grey eyes as he tried again: 'How would nine hundred and fifty thousand pounds sound? I mean, don't you find this house too large to manage? You could cut down on your outgoings extensively if you found yourself a lovely new modern home.'

She really was enjoying watching him cough and stutter.

'I mean, not that your home is not lovely,' he went on.

She could see that he was vastly over-talking and quite out of his depth. She sat there seething whilst the dreadful man continued to make a complete ass of himself, until finally she exploded.

'What could you possibly know about my finances? How dare you presume to tell me what is best for me. You, an absolute stranger!' Without even considering what she had just been told, she rudely went on, 'I have no intention of leaving this house until it's feet first in a box. Now, if you will excuse me, I have better things to do with my time than to talk to a schoolboy with ideas above his station.'

'But, Mrs Watson, please hear me out. This could be a most wonderful opportunity for you, and I'm sure my wife would allow me to improve on my offer. You see, my wife's mother has not been well, and we need something large enough to enable us to have her live with us and yet still enable us all to have our independence.'

This struck a chord with Edna, remembering how her mother had first come to live with them during a most unhappy time in her mother's life. This was a period of which she didn't want to be reminded, and so she decided that she had wasted enough time listening to Mr Clitheroe. It was time for him to go.

Edna marched past him into the hallway and opened the front door, indicating to the bewildered man that the meeting was over. Totally bemused, he made a rapid retreat down the drive. Perceptive as ever, she knew that something about his story just didn't feel right.

As soon as he was out of sight, Edward Clitheroe called his boss. 'Bad news, I'm afraid, Reg. She's not in the slightest interested.'

'Well, we shall have to find a way to convince her, won't we? Time to call in Franklyn,' his boss replied.

The third, yet unwilling, person in the unscrupulous team plotting to finagle Edna out of her house was her bank manager, Toby Franklyn, who was often heard referring to Edna as 'that terrible woman'. It had been so very easy to blackmail Franklyn into doing what they wanted, which was to help them get that valuable land that Edna Watson was sitting on. Once Edward had found out that Franklyn was being a naughty boy, cheating on his wife with Margaret, the buxom blonde from the estate agents, it had not been difficult to get him to do what he wanted, and from then on, Edward's bullying had been relentless. He had wasted no time in threatening the pitiful man that he needed to get this right if he wanted to keep his love interest happy and his wife blissfully unaware of what was going on.

Edward had made him aware that his role in the corrupt affair was to get her to agree to come into the bank so that he could convince her that her finances were not in the healthy state she imagined and that it would be prudent to sell up and buy a smaller place.

'Don't worry, Reg, I'll see to it.' And he dialled again.

'Good morning, FNC.'

'Morning, Edward Clitheroe for Toby Franklyn.' He heard the phone click.

'Good morning, Edward, what can I do for you?'

'She hasn't taken the bait, so it's time for you to take over.'

Edward could feel Franklyn's uneasiness, but he just didn't care. Edward was sure that Franklyn had hoped the blasted woman would take the offer and that his part would be superfluous to needs, but no such luck.

'I – I'm not sure that I'm going to be any good at this,' Franklyn stammered weakly.

'Now, stop all this nonsense. You know what will happen if you don't call her, so I suggest that you just get on with it.' As far as Edward was concerned, the conversation was over, and the phone went dead.

❧

After her encounter with the oh-so-common Mr Clitheroe, Edna busied herself making a cup of tea, which she carried into the sitting room along with a couple of custard creams. She sat mulling over the conversation. Don's careful planning had ensured that Edna was well provided for, but she didn't want to spend anything. After he died, she had just lost interest in everything, particularly money. What on earth would she have done with all that money if she sold the house, she pondered. *Give it to my two daughters? Not ruddy likely.* She thought about how such a large amount of money could change her life: cruises to far-off lands, a new modern, easy-to-keep-clean flat in one of those fancy blocks they were building along the towpath. *Knock yourself out, Edna, and live like a queen. And what? Leave the only house that Don and I have ever lived in?* So she had thought about the offer for less than five minutes and then jokingly thought that maybe she had better lie down in a darkened room until the madness had passed.

Edna was particularly edgy and irritated because she realised that Edward Clitheroe had reminded her of a time that she would rather forget. She thought about Felicity's call. Would she, could she, turn her uncle's death to her advantage? She could never wipe out the years of misery and insecurity, but she might just feel better if she finally vented her anger and let her aunt have it. She had still not definitely made up her mind and needed to give it more thought, but it was certainly a possibility, she admitted to herself. If she were just brave enough to do it.

She turned her attention back to Don. Throughout their marriage she had always avoided being dependent upon Don, hoping that it would help her cope better if he left her. Well, leave her he did, but not in the way that she had feared. She could never have imagined that her dread of losing him would manifest itself so cruelly. Don, the man that she had loved so ardently, and lost. Without warning, on what had started out as a beautiful September day, Edna had suffered the most devastating blow of all. One minute they were chatting away about nothing in particular, and the next, Don was choking violently on a chicken bone. She had tried to perform the Heimlich manoeuvre (not that she had ever been trained to do so), as she had watched it many times on *Casualty* and *Holby City*. It was all hopeless though. The ambulance driver, wanting to comfort her, had said that it was so fast, her beloved Don would not have suffered for long.

She desperately wanted to believe that, but she still had that vision of him gasping for breath so violently, and she knew that the look of panic on his face and the devil's grip in her stomach would never leave her.

I mean, it's not as if we were stupidly in love like you see on those American TV shows, she said to herself, *but it was love in our own funny, comfortable way, even if we did yell at each other. Correction. I yelled at him, and he just sat there looking bewildered, like a little boy who had been admonished by his mother for swearing but didn't know what he had done wrong.*

Turning her attention to the *Daily Mail,* she read the paper from cover to cover until her rumbling stomach reminded her that it was lunchtime.

She entered the kitchen, heated a can of her favourite tomato soup, and toasted some sourdough bread (one of the few things about modern life that she did enjoy), buttering it liberally. She sat at the kitchen table, cradling her mug of soup in the house that she and Don had shared together for thirty years.

Built in the 1800s, tucked away in a country lane leading nowhere, the house was surrounded by beautiful countryside, with no chance of prying visitors, which suited Edna just fine. It stood with its red-pitched tiled roof set against the white stucco façade, with a brown oak door and tell-tale signs where once had been an arch of luscious roses. Such lovely scented, peachy pink blooms that had permeated the whole house. The beautiful garden, once lovingly tended by Don, was now overgrown with weeds and grass so high she could no longer sit there. *What's the point? It rains more than it shines.* The wishing well in the front garden, once a source of great fun and hope, had not heard a request for years. At the end of the garden was the potting shed where Don had spent hours sorting brooms, pots, irrigation tools and even seeds until the mice had discovered them.

Once so lovingly maintained, the inside of the house had not been touched since Don had departed. The once-brilliant white paint was now a stale shade of yellow. The girls' bedrooms remained empty and unloved since they had left for university. Having found their mother so difficult, they never returned to live at Rose Cottage, preferring to rent a room until they had managed to save a deposit for their own home. The sofas were rubbed and tired, with deep caverns where cushions were once full and firm, yet Edna, racked with back pain, refused to get them re-stuffed. *Waste of money,* she would say to herself. *No one comes to visit, my toffee-nosed daughters only come twice a month, and I hardly ever see the grandchildren, so why bother?*

The house was perfectly positioned for someone who had never driven. Within a five-minute walk she could be at the health centre, a general shop with basics, and a village hall. *Aaaargh! All those WI do-gooders. Not for me!*

Even after the tomato soup, Edna was still hungry and wanted to get the awful scene of Don taking his last breath out of her head. She opened the freezer and selected a cheese and tomato pizza and placed it in the oven. *Yes, that should do it. It will remind me about our honeymoon in Venice.*

Whilst she waited for it to be ready, she went back into the sitting room and selected a photograph album. As she turned the pages, her eyes became moist, looking at all the happy moments, and she had to admit that as hard as life had been to her, there were some pretty wonderful times too. There were photos of Edna gazing up at Don while he delivered his wedding speech. She and Don on the canal with a friendly gondolier. On a Riva speeding along with her hair flying in the spray. Edna with a mouthful of gelato, a most delighted look upon her face. Don with a cushion under his shirt standing side by side with Edna while emulating her pregnancy. Olivia and Viola in the garden jumping in the water arc created by the hose. Standing in the iconic pose outside the Taj Mahal. Sitting in a helicopter about to take off from a blue glacier. About to board a seaplane to visit the fjords. There were pages and pages of wonderful and happy times, but then, very abruptly, they had stopped. Don had left her and that flaming chicken bone had ensured that there would be no more happy memories.

The timer pinged, alerting her to her waiting pizza, and she went back into the kitchen and greedily consumed the doughy bread that was topped with just a smattering of tomato and cheese and bore little resemblance to the real thing.

With all the talk of the past and Edward Clitheroe's innocent comment about his mother-in-law, Edna was feeling deeply troubled. The man had unwittingly reminded her of a most unhappy time when her own mother had come to live with her and Don, and despite all her irresolution about reading the book, inquisitiveness took over. It seemed that today was to be a day of decisions, and Edna was thinking that maybe it was time to try to put the past at rest. There were two ways she felt she could achieve that. The first was to draw on her courage to attend her uncle's funeral, and the second was to be brave enough to open the box. So, trembling and nervous, she made her way upstairs. She reached up and took hold of the box, laid it on the bed and as carefully as she could, with hands that would have registered five on the Richter scale, she removed the book inside. She stared at the cover for a long time, unable to open it.

'What am I so scared of, Don? What could possibly be there that terrifies me so?'

Finally, with a burst of bravery that in truth she did not feel, she placed it carefully under her arm and went back downstairs, feeling ready to confront the past. She gingerly opened it to the first page, but before her eyes could focus on the words, the phone rang, jolting Edna back to the present. Her fingers recoiled from the box as it if were molten lava, and she rushed to pick up the phone.

'4742,' Edna announced.

'Hello, Edna. Me again.'

Edna felt her hackles rise and, wanting to avoid another conversation with her cousin, invented an excuse for not speaking. 'Yes, Felicity, you'll have to speak up as I have an important appointment to attend.'

'We are hoping that there is no need for a postmortem, and so the funeral is set for Friday week at two o'clock. Mother says that she has not heard from you, but I said that she had probably missed the call and to check her messages.'

She hasn't heard from me because I haven't called her. Gosh, you can be stupid, Edna wanted to yell at Felicity, but instead, gritting her teeth, she politely replied, 'You will have to forgive me, but I have to answer the door.' Then, unable to stop herself, she continued, 'Unfortunately for you, you do seem to call at the most inconvenient times.' Edna replaced the receiver without even saying goodbye.

Having got rid of her annoying cousin by feigning a visitor, Edna returned to the sitting room and the book.

She was soon to find out that the book would become more precious to her than the finest Sevres porcelain. As she slowly caressed it, feeling her mother's energy, she at last dared to open it again.

Then, totally engrossed and in utter disbelief at what she discovered, she started to read the journal and was completely spellbound by her mother's surprising and often shocking story.

❧

1st December 1965

Something wonderful happened today. I met William (Bill) whilst walking round the Royal Academy. Having dropped my scarf without noticing, I felt a tap on my shoulder. I looked up into the most beautiful piercing blue eyes and wondered what on earth he could want.

'Excuse me, but I think you dropped this.' His voice had an air of Gregory Peck about it, and I felt my heart quicken.

'Thank you, err, yes, this is mine,' I simpered in response, sounding I'm sure like the heroine in a Barbara Cartland novel, as I clasped hold of my Hermes silk chiffon scarf, printed with a delicate pale sea of animals. I felt myself blushing profusely whilst something stirred inside of me, a feeling that I had not experienced for many years, and I felt so guilty just at the feelings arousing me so. We had both been looking at 'Central Park New York' by Charles Cundall. We chatted about its merits and whether we enjoyed it, and he asked me to join him for a coffee. I knew that I should say no, but the intensity of the feelings that I was experiencing compelled me to say yes. He introduced himself over coffee and biscuits and I learned that he lived in Central Park, hence his interest in the painting.

His wife, although still alive, was in a vegetative state, in the last throes of what had been diagnosed years ago as early-onset Alzheimer's. He had kept her at home for as long as he could, but she was now unable to care for herself in any way, and tragically had become very aggressive and violent. Despite the great sums he was prepared to pay, it became impossible to convince her carers to stay, and so reluctantly he had finally made the rounds looking for a well-run facility. He told me that she was extremely well looked after in an ultra-luxurious American residential home with full medical care.

I, in turn, told him about my loveless marriage with a man who had turned out to be such a disappointment.

I studied Bill's handsome face, framed by a shock of blonde hair, and acknowledged that even in the best days with your father, Richard,

I had never ever felt like this. We talked about our love of art and our families. He with an eighteen-year-old son at Yale and me with my twelve-year-old daughter (you), and I told him that you were the only reason that I stayed with your father.

Although we both knew it was terribly wrong, we agreed to meet at the Academy the following week. What harm could there be in that? I thought. It's not as if I were making an arrangement to meet in some sordid hotel bedroom. Of course, I knew that my reasoning didn't make it right, but I was happier than I had been my whole life, and I could not stop.

⌒

Edna was completely poleaxed at this revelation, there never having been a hint of impropriety in any of the family marriages. She wondered if she should read on, but her compulsion to know what happened impelled her to continue. She reasoned that her mother would have destroyed the journal if she hadn't wanted Edna to read her innermost thoughts. As Iris's story unfolded, Edna could see that her mother had written it for her. Even today, so many years after Iris had written it, Edna was unsettled to read her mother's most intimate revelations, and she felt distinctly uncomfortable as she turned the pages.

⌒

5th *January 1966*

This past month of 'harmless' meetings has been like a dream. Coffees on a bench in Hyde Park, visits to the flower market in Covent Garden, meals in the suburbs of London that we felt would not be inhabited by people we knew. As time has gone on, our meetings have now given way to urgent kisses each time we part. Yesterday it finally did become an afternoon of passion, but there was absolutely nothing sordid about it. I have never felt so loved, so safe, so completely and utterly adored. There's no going back now. We have to find a way to be together. I am wracked with guilt, never having contemplated being with another man, but my marriage with Richard has been unhappy for so many years now and I want to grasp this chance to be happy. But what of you, Edna, how can I put my happiness before yours? I have to be first and foremost a mother, don't I?

Edna gulped. She actually could not believe that this was her mother talking. Her nervous, very correct, extremely loveable, but weak mother was showing a side of her character that was totally unrecognisable, and the image of Iris in a steamy affair was extremely hard to comprehend. Since she had been with Don, Edna had never looked at another man longingly, let alone entertained the idea of extramarital relations. Her mother having sex, even with her father, was just not something she had ever wanted to think about. To contemplate the scenario with another man - well, that was a step too far.

Stirring from her thoughts, Edna realised that it was seven o'clock and so she placed the book carefully back on the coffee table and prepared her supper.

Reluctantly, as Edna could not abide waste, she accepted that she had to cook the chops tonight. She seasoned yesterday's abandoned meat, washed the new potatoes, dropped a handful of mint into the saucepan and started cooking. She grilled the chops, swallowing hard at the thought of having to wash the greasy grill-pan, steamed the potatoes, added the vegetables for the last five minutes and finally, even though she was far more curious to get back to her mother's journal, she sat down to enjoy her supper. After devouring it, having scraped her plate of every last morsel, she moved to the sink to wash up.

'Listen, Don, I know that it's time for *Who Wants to be a Millionaire?* and we do love that, don't we, but if you don't mind, I want to miss it tonight. I finally found the courage to open my mother's book today and it's proving to be worse than I thought. She had an affair! Can you imagine? Mummy sleeping with a man other than Daddy. Well, of course you couldn't. I can tell you that she has rocked me to the core. There is so much to read, and I just might end up burning the midnight oil.'

Yet again Edna was sad and disappointed at the lack of response from Don and the hollow empty sound of the house.

She decided that she would rather carry on reading in bed and so she went to the biscuit tin, stuck her slightly podgy fingers into the well, pulled out two custard creams and placed them carefully in her pocket.

Again, feeling slightly anxious about the conversation with Edward Clitheroe, although she couldn't quite put her finger on why, she made herself a hot chocolate and climbed the stairs, gently patting her pocket to assure herself that her biscuits were indeed there. Tucking the journal under her arm, she took it upstairs and looked sadly around her bedroom, wondering if she would ever find pleasure in it again.

Once more, she spoke to the lonely room.

'It's just so lonely without you, Don.' Edna sighed as she placed the hot chocolate down on the bedside table, laid her biscuits on a paper hankie, removed her clothes, placed her underwear in the laundry bin and hung her outer clothes to air. She pulled a nightie over her head and then brushed her hair, making a mental note to brush her teeth later. She then settled into bed to savour her midnight feast, which would hopefully soothe the gaping wound that the book was carving into her chest.

She opened it and carefully turned the pages, making sure not to get crumbs in her precious book.

෴

9th March 1966

Today Bill has asked me to go to New York and start a new life with him. Tempting as it is, I am not sure how I could go with him. How could I uproot you, Edna, and take you to another country away from your beloved father and expect you to make new friends, start a new school and leave everything behind that was safe and good? We are beginning to realise that the thought of life without each other is intolerable and are trying to devise a plan that could work. Maybe if we took the year in bite-size pieces? Bill could well afford to ferry us back and forth across the Atlantic, and he has suggested that if I were to leave you in London for just one month at a time, maybe it could work? I know that I can't do that, but nevertheless, we are going to explore all options.

Bill has suggested that we go to New York and see if I could imagine myself living there and we have decided to try the first of our dry runs, just to see how I might fit into Manhattan life. We are flying to New York for a long weekend in July and I am telling Richard that I have been invited on a hen trip with an old school friend.

I feel excruciatingly guilty leaving you at home, Edna, and in truth, even guilty at deceiving Richard. He has not proved to be the husband that he promised to be, and I know that I have to grab the chance with both hands. I have half convinced myself that you would be OK and that maybe even the break would do us both good. You seem to prefer Richard to me and always focus on what I have done wrong. Maybe it's a mother-daughter thing, but it still hurts. He does so little for you, and yet he is the one you always run to and side with.

෴

Edna felt a pang of guilt as she realised how unfair she had been to her mother. If only she could have turned the clock back; with hindsight, she would have shown her mother just how much she adored her. And so, with a heart full of lead, she continued to read.

∾

22nd July 1966

Last night I tossed and turned, unable to sleep, hardly able to contain my excitement that our plans for New York have become a reality. Richard lay next to me peacefully sleeping, totally unaware of the life-changing events that might ensue after the 'reunion with my friend' in New York.

Realising that I was not going to fall asleep, I gave in and wandered around our home filled with beautiful memories of better times, treasured photos of loved ones long passed, books and ornaments, all with a story to tell, like the bronze hand holding a heart we had found in St Paul de Vence on our fifth wedding anniversary, the much-loved chair in the spare bedroom where I nursed you, Edna, the dining table with the annoying scratch that only I know is there and the markings inside the pantry as your growth was recorded. If I leave Richard, this beautiful house is surely going to have to be sold. We will have to budget to buy two homes in a lesser area for sure, which is not going to be easy as I'm sure that you won't like it, especially as while you're so young I won't tell you my reason for leaving him. I don't want to be the one responsible for showing you his feet of clay, so this will be just another reason for you to feel sorry for Richard and angry with me.

It's now five in the morning, and I check my handbag one more time. Bill and I have agreed to go separately to the airport and not to acknowledge each other until we are on board, just in case we bump into anyone that either of us knows.

25ᵗʰ *July 1966*

The taxi arrived and as it whisked me off to Heathrow, I wondered what Richard would say if he knew that I was travelling first class. Here I was, on an adventure like no other, and I couldn't tell another living soul about it. The driver dropped me at the terminal, and I nervously checked in. I felt like a celebrity with all the kowtowing. It was just another world.

Sitting in the first-class lounge, I felt like a teenager again, wrapped in a heady swirl of electrifying shots running through my body. I buried my head in a book, reading the same line over and over again, lest I look up and see him, because if anyone had seen my eyes, they would have seen an intensity of passion that would have given the game away for sure. I forced myself to stay calm, and then finally came the announcement, and I boarded the BOAC Comet jet to New York, again making sure not to look at my fellow passengers just in case we locked eyes. My heart was taking another bashing, and I was trying to control my breathing. I don't think that I could ever remember feeling so excited and panicked all at the same time. I had never flown first class before, and I nervously offered what was now my slightly dog-eared boarding pass. I had been so nervous running my fingers over it again and again. The stewardess ushered me to my seat and there, before me, sitting in 1A, I saw this most magnificent man smiling at me with those bright blue eyes. I was so happy in the knowledge that, for at least the next seventy-two hours, he was mine and I was his. Tears of happiness were rolling down my cheeks, and when he took my hand, I truly thought that I was going to pass out from sheer elation.

A steward offered me a glass of champagne, Dom Perignon no less, accompanied by a selection of canapés consisting of foie gras, smoked salmon and caviar. Bill and I toasted each other and dared to dream of what could hopefully be our amazing future. An hour later, I could hardly believe my eyes when the steward returned with a silver trolley.

He opened the dome and there was the most delicious-looking side of roast beef, roast potatoes and a selection of vegetables.

'May I offer you the roast beef, or would you prefer the lobster?'

I opted for the beef whilst he continued with the endless choices. Would I like a little gravy? Oh yes, I would, thank you. Was this really how people lived? I was completely overwhelmed.

Finally we landed, and as we disembarked the aircraft, there was a man holding a board with Bill's name on it. We were whisked through security and out into the sunlight where our limousine was waiting for us. Our driver's name was Garfield, and he was quite literally a gentle giant. He and Bill hugged each other, and then he offered me a strong and warm handshake, and I liked him immediately. He ushered me into a stretch limousine, the likes of which I had never seen. He offered me a glass of champagne. Just imagine a glass of champagne in a car! Bill looked at me in wonderment and later told me that I had looked so vulnerable, like a little girl let loose in the candy store. He had thoughtfully rented an apartment so that we did not suffer the embarrassment of bumping into someone in a hotel lobby.

The concierge smiled at us and motioned to a bell boy to take our luggage up to the apartment, which was on the 47th floor looking out over Manhattan. The view out onto 63rd and 3rd was magnificent, with all the cars like twinkling stars lighting up the beautiful city, the memory of which brings tears to my eyes even now.

We had barely got through the door when Bill grabbed me and kissed me with such fervour. I wouldn't let go of him because I didn't want the moment to end. I am sure that one day you, Edna, are going to find this, and so I will keep my memories of our lovemaking safely locked away in my head.

❧

At this revelation, Edna squirmed.

᳇

Suffice to say that eventually we rolled out of bed, because, albeit jet-lagged and slightly woolly, I just had to walk the streets. I found that I truly came alive in the city of endless possibilities, where Bill told me that miracles could happen. I desperately hoped that he was right and that we could find happiness together without destroying the lives of those that we loved.

Manhattan was beyond thrilling, with the steam rising from underground, the flashing Walk/Don't Walk traffic signs, the hotdog stalls that I could smell from a mile away, all giving out that energy that I craved. Eventually my shoes gave up, and rather than wait for Garfield, I wanted to go in a yellow taxi. We took a heart-stopping, take-your-life-in-your-hands cab ride back to the apartment, and after screeching to a halt, the driver in his Bronx accent said, 'OK, folks, this is it. Sixty toid 'n toid,' and we both fell about laughing.

The weekend was just amazing. We lit a candle at St Patrick's on 5th Avenue, and then enjoyed a romantic dinner at the River Café lying under the shadow of Brooklyn Bridge. The following day we had lunch at the Tavern on the Green with its twinkling glass room right in the centre of Central Park, and that night we savoured the famous Beef Wellington at One if by Land Two if by Sea. The beautiful room with candlelit tables, two fireplaces, and a baby grand piano took my breath away. The following day we lunched on bagels and lox (smoked salmon to us Brits) at Russ and Daughters in Houston Street and an early supper at the Rainbow Room, hoping for a glance of Cary Grant or Gore Vidal. Sadly, the moments at the Met, Central Park, Statue of Liberty, Ellis Island, Broadway, Little Italy, China Town and Empire State all slipped away far too quickly and long before I was ready, it was time for me reluctantly to return to my life with Richard.

Throughout the journey home, we frantically discussed how to make it work, but the answer was always the same. I couldn't leave you, Edna.

Bill couldn't leave his wife, and that meant we had to come up with a miracle.

Even the heat that was by now raging through Edna's body was not enough to keep her awake. Her mind and her body were both completely exhausted and so she closed the book, turned out the light and within moments she was fast asleep.

CHAPTER THREE

Thursday

EDNA WOKE EARLY, pulled her dressing gown around her and, holding the journal carefully under her arm, went downstairs. With nothing specially planned she was looking forward to having an undisturbed morning reading more of her mother's unbelievable story. She burnt her tongue swallowing the hot tea too quickly and gobbled her breakfast of bran flakes and banana without savouring a bite, all of which was so unlike her, but she couldn't wait to get back to reading.

After clearing the crumbs from the table, she was about to go upstairs to draw her bath, but yet again she was disturbed by a phone call. At this point she was now really irritable, and these days it didn't take much to make her so. Although she didn't really understand the difference, this was a WhatsApp call on her mobile phone. Edna detested all this new technology, but her daughters insisted that for security's sake, it was a necessary evil. Groaning under her breath at the sheer inconvenience of having to talk to another person and hoping that it was not going to turn out to be another day of unwanted disturbances, she pressed the button.

'Hello,' she said absent-mindedly, whilst moving upstairs. For all her protestations about the mobile phone, she had to admit that it made things easier when she could press the loudspeaker button and carry on with tasks while speaking on the phone.

'Hello, Mrs Watson, it's Franklyn here, from the bank.'

After Don had died, Edna had changed banks because she loved the dog that was part of their advertisement. Don would never have sanctioned a move to a bank based upon a dog, *but then Don isn't here, is he!* She moved into the bedroom and placed the phone on a shelf whilst she removed her nightie. The man chatted away and then…

'Err, I think you're on video!' poor Mr Franklyn nervously declared.

Horrified at this exclamation, Edna was frantically trying to work out which button to push. In her haste to cut him off, she actually made matters worse, unable to end the call whilst her bosoms were flopping about over the screen. In desperation she turned the phone face down, leaving the poor, embarrassed man to disconnect the call.

Mortified by her carelessness, Edna was now preoccupied thinking about how to resolve this horrendous situation. *No,* she decided. *There have been quite enough interruptions for today. I'm going to have my bath and I'll sort it out tomorrow.*

The powerful aroma took over once more and against her better wishes, she found herself once more wrestling with her thoughts about going to the funeral.

Come on, Edna, pull yourself together. This is not going to solve anything. She abandoned the bath and stepped out, dried herself quickly, pulled on her fleece and joggers, and made her way downstairs. She rinsed her mug and after making another strong cup of tea, she settled down in the sitting room to open the book again, but still agitated by old wounds, her mind wandered and she stressed about her unwitting exposure of her intimate body parts to Mr Franklyn. The unfortunate conversation was still very much playing on her mind. *Why did he call me? I don't even know what he wanted.* Edna's heart was racing. She finally decided that the best plan of action was to call the bank and close her account. There was no way that she could stay there after such a mortifyingly embarrassing experience.

She was quite adept at the computer, having taught herself after Don died. It was just another skill that she had been forced to learn after he had deserted her. She sat down, opened Google and typed, 'HOW TO CLOSE A BACK ACCOUNT'.

Much to her dismay, there it was, the answer that she didn't want:

'To carry out the account closure process, an account holder needs to visit the branch personally. At the branch, you need to submit an account closure form along with the de-linking form, unused cheque book and debit card. In the form, you need to mention the reason for the closure of the bank account.'

Edna was furious. *Not only do I have to visit the bank, I have to think of something else to put on the form because I'm hardly likely to put 'because the manager saw my bosoms!'* She was done for; there it was in black and white. It said that she had to attend. Horrified at the prospect, she called the bank, hoping to get them to agree to the closure by post.

'I'm really sorry, madam, but you will have to come in personally if you want to close your account and transfer funds to another bank.'

If Edna had not known better, she could have sworn that the girl was enjoying this. Had that wretched Franklyn told everyone? Given them a good laugh, at her expense? Edna felt sick, her hands clammy, desperately trying to work out how she was going to resolve this and still keep face.

'I am sixty-nine and I don't drive, so I will thank you to take my instructions over the telephone.'

'Just a moment, please, and let me see what I can do.'

Edna was frustrated and angrily tapped her unpolished nails (*just too much trouble to paint them unless I have somewhere important to go*) on the hall table. *How much longer is she going to keep me hanging on, listening to that dreadful muzak? Heaven help me!*

∼

Franklyn had been sitting at his desk fuming. It was such a nuisance that the call was messed up by that stupid woman exposing herself. Quite put him off his lunch! He was on a not-inconsequential retainer from Trident, the local property developers, due to the fact that they had discovered that he had got himself into a spot of bother, cheating on his wife with Margaret from the estate agents. Now Margaret had an insatiable appetite for designer handbags, sparkly jewellery and, just lately, a deposit on a new flat in the latest Trident development.

As he sat there going over the morning's unfortunate events, his anger soon turned to despair. *I don't even know how Edward Clitheroe discovered what's been going on. How can I scare Edna Watson about her future finances and advise her that the most prudent and sensible thing to do would be to find a buyer for her house when she won't even talk to me?*

No, he fumed, closing her account because of that wretched WhatsApp call was not in the plan at all. He had to acknowledge that if he was to get Clitheroe off his back, he must scare the woman into selling her house, but now she had unknowingly thwarted the opportunity. So when young Linda came in and announced that Mrs Watson wanted to close her account and was refusing to come in, he seized his chance. The wretched woman had played right into his hands. The plan was back on again! He rubbed his hands together and told Linda that he would personally take the papers to her house.

⨏

Finally, Edna heard the young woman come back on the line.

'I have spoken to Mr Franklyn, and he says that in this instance he would be more than happy to bring the papers to your house where he could formalise everything.'

Edna felt herself go weak at the knees. *Come face to face with the man who had been privy to the sight of my naked breasts? Not frigging likely!*

'That will not be necessary,' Edna barked. 'I will be there at twelve-thirty tomorrow morning,' and promptly slammed the receiver down. Starving again, she went into the kitchen and made herself a salmon paste sandwich.

It was still troubling her that she didn't even know why Mr Franklyn had called this morning.

Apart from the horrendous embarrassment the call had caused, Edna realised that reluctantly she had to part association with that beautiful dog. It also occurred to her that however embarrassing the call was, it placed her right up there with the legendary Dame Judi Dench and Charles Saatchi. She remembered having read in the newspaper of their involuntary naked appearances on something called Facetime. Not that Edna would have wanted to be connected with *that Saatchi man*, but she would have felt in very good company with Dame Judi. *Such a lady.* Of course, Edna didn't subscribe to Facetime. She didn't even know what it was, but she had enjoyed a jolly good belly laugh when she read about it in the *Daily Mail.* Now though, when it was about accidentally exposing herself… well, that was quite another matter. This most mortifying experience just added to the secretiveness that had been a recurring theme in Edna's life.

The calls from her cousin were still playing heavily on Edna's mind. They had really upset her, and she was now feeling slightly cranky and more than a little tired, not to mention hungry again. She collected the newspaper, made herself a mug of tea and carried it upstairs to her bedroom with a couple of bourbon biscuits tucked in behind her napkin for an afternoon snack. She planned to allow herself the luxury of an hour's rest on the bed, but then, agitated by old wounds, her mind wandered. She was still shaken and stressed about her unwitting exposure to Mr Franklyn and became obsessed with her appointment the following day. She had to resolve the embarrassing situation with him. One that she most certainly could not, would not, ever reveal to anyone.

Sighing heavily, Edna opened her mother's journal.

ᴥ

28th August 1966

Ironically, only last month I was convinced I couldn't leave Richard for the chance to run off and live in New York, embarking upon a potentially rocky stab at a new and exciting life with Bill. No, I decided, after weeks of heart-wrenching discussions with myself, I did not have the courage to leave Richard because I would not be able to take away his beloved daughter. I certainly couldn't live without you, Edna, who I have to accept would never want to leave your father anyway, so I conceded that I would just stay with my boring and sometimes miserable life, so far removed from that which I had planned all those years ago.

Then something monumental happened. Having left you downstairs to get ready for your long-awaited 13th birthday party, Richard and I moved into the bedroom. He sat me down on the bed and instinctively I tried to stand up again. I don't know why, maybe it was the way he was picking at the tips of his fingers, the way that he always did when he was nervous, but I just knew that something awful was coming.

'Please don't get up, I need to talk to you.'

'I've had such a busy day getting everything ready for Edna; I'm exhausted. Can't this wait until tomorrow?' I said irritably.

'No, this has to be now, before I lose my nerve,' he implored.

I started to feel anxious, and an uncomfortable thought came rushing into my head. Had he found out what my plan had been? Please not now, not when I had decided to stay. Despite being irreligious, I found myself praying to a higher force. Of course, nothing could have prepared me for what followed.

Richard stared at the floor and slowly raised his head. I could see that he was crying.

'I've been gambling for most of our married life, but it is now out of control, and not only have we run out of money, but I'm being prosecuted for misappropriating clients' funds, as well as owing the Revenue taxes, which we cannot afford to pay. I love you and Edna and would do anything to save our marriage. I want to make this right, so I've found out about an association called Gamblers Anonymous that could help us. I want to go and want you to please come with me,' he pleaded.

'We? We? Who is the "we" in all of this?' I screamed at him. 'I haven't gambled. I haven't run out of money. I haven't misappropriated clients' funds. I don't owe the taxman money,' I snarled. 'Don't you drag me into this. What the hell is Gamblers Anonymous anyway?'

Whatever it was he was trying to pull me into, I didn't want it. It was bad enough that I was going to have to lose Bill, but I was not going to be dragged into Richard's disgusting financial affairs.

The coward then went into the spare bedroom and closed the door, leaving me completely bereft.

Hours later, you came upstairs to bed, Edna. You walked into the bedroom and saw my face, ravaged and raw. You asked me what the matter was, and I'm ashamed to say that without asking how your party went, I launched into a tirade about Richard and his gambling. You screamed at me and then, covering your ears, ran into your bedroom.

❧

At this point in her mother's story, Edna stopped and recalled the events of her thirteenth birthday all too well.

At twelve years of age, Edna felt that her whole world centred around her crush on Michael Eden. He was just the most gorgeous thing she had ever seen. Michael had a dark Paul McCartney bob and twinkling eyes. She would spend hours giggling with Daisy, fantasising about her upcoming party and becoming Michael's girl-friend. She and Daisy were planning what she should wear on what Edna imagined would be the most exciting night of her life. They finally settled on a shocking pink Polly Peck shift of slub silk, with a little Peter Pan collar and pleated front with matching covered silk buttons down the centre.

'I don't think that he will be able to leave you alone in that,' said Daisy in a mock Marlene Dietrich pose, with voice to match, where-upon they had both fallen onto the bed in a fit of giggles. Visually they were complete opposites. Edna was dark-haired with penetrat-ing eyes, and Daisy had wispy blonde hair and huge Twiggy-style fluttering eyelashes. They were both the same size and were always swapping clothes.

There was a big struggle underway with Richard because he would not let Edna wear any makeup, so the plan was that Iris would leave some makeup downstairs, and as soon as Iris and Richard had made their way upstairs and out of the way, Daisy would help Edna beautify herself. The challenge was to get Richard upstairs before the guests arrived. It was decided that they would tell Richard that the party started thirty minutes earlier than it was actually due to start to give Edna time to get ready.

'But I want to greet your guests,' Richard protested.

'Oh, Daddy, that's so old-fashioned. No one does that anymore,' she giggled and gave him a big bear hug. 'And absolutely no peeking! I don't want to be embarrassed!'

Finally, the long-awaited day arrived and having safely seen her father upstairs, she and Daisy rushed into the cloakroom and set about applying her makeup. First came the foundation.

'Just a touch,' said Daisy. 'You don't want to look like you've spent a month in Majorca!' At this, they both started laughing again. Next, Daisy deftly applied a sprinkling of pink rouge, and finally a little Max Factor mascara for which she had to get Edna to spit on the black block, after which she rubbed the little black brush back and forth and then applied the goo to Edna's eyelashes. Daisy stood back to survey her handiwork.

'Edna, you look amazing. He can't help but fall.'

Famous last words. They moved into the hallway and waited to greet Edna's guests. One by one everyone arrived, but not Michael. Edna was anxiously looking at the door, willing him to appear, and she was not enjoying her party one little bit. Friends tried to talk to her, but she was just answering in monosyllables. Eventually, people stopped trying and just enjoyed the party. Then, an hour late, Michael sauntered in, greeting everyone along the way. Eventually, they came face to face.

'Happy Birthday,' he said most unenthusiastically, pushing a box of Cadbury Milk Tray into her hands. With that far-from-romantic greeting, he turned and launched himself into the arms of a giggly blonde. They spent an hour dancing, and then he left. Edna's antici-pated romance had turned out to be an enormous disappointment. It was clear that Michael, who had arrived late and left early, was not the least bit interested in Edna, and she had felt so let down because she had been convinced for many years that her life was going to change when she reached that magic number. Well, life did change, but not in a good way. Sad and deflated after the non-event party, Edna had walked into the bathroom to find her mother crying.

'What's the matter?' Edna asked grudgingly. She had already had enough misery for one evening, her birthday being such a let-down and, to add insult to injury, her mother was putting a dampener on everything.

'Your father is a gambler. He's been losing money for years, but now the money has run out, and we have absolutely nothing.'

If Iris had been talking in Swahili, Edna could not have been more confused. She remembered asking herself why her mother had chosen that moment to tell her. Didn't she know it was her thirteenth birthday and that she absolutely *did not* want to hear it, not that day, in fact, not ever? She didn't want to hear anything bad about her daddy. He was her hero, the person she loved more than anything in the world, even more than Michael Eden. Still a child at heart, Edna put her hands over her ears and ran out of the room. Looking back now, she wondered how she could have been so heartless as to not try to comfort her mother. True to form, she was just a selfish teenager who was only concerned with her own happiness.

12th September 1966

For some crazy reason I felt that I had to accompany Richard to a meeting at least once and so I decided to find out what I could about this so-called GA. I learned that this was a brand new and revolutionary association formed to try to combat gambling, whilst offering support not only to the gamblers but also to their families. Looking back, I have no idea why I agreed to go, but I suppose I felt that I owed him at least that.

We drove in silence, and I just wanted the evening to be over. We pulled up outside what appeared to be a derelict building but was, in fact, an old community hall in Lambeth. With a heart filled with lead I walked in behind Richard and was overwhelmed by a sea of faces. Old, young, men, women, a variety of all shapes and sizes. Some looked like vagrants, and some looked like they were on their way to their job in the city. It was a complete melange. Then a hush came over the hall and everyone stood.

'God grant me the serenity to accept the things I cannot change, the courage to change the things I can, and the wisdom to know the difference.'

Everyone was chanting what I discovered was a mantra that started every meeting. I looked around the room listening to all these strangers and wondered what on earth I was doing there. I was absolutely horrified by the stories I heard that night. The first man stood, looking like a puffed-up canary. He started in the traditional way for all gamblers to begin:

'My name is Greg, and I am a compulsive gambler.' He explained that he had been a gambler for most of his life and had not admitted the truth until he had not only run out of money but had also racked up serious debts that he couldn't repay. One of the creditors was the Inland Revenue. The coward had not told his wife anything and had not even pre-warned her of what was going on. Even on the morning of his court appearance for tax evasion he had kissed her goodbye, dressed in his usual suit and tie, pretending to go to work as he had done for the last three months, and closed the front door. The first she knew of anything was when the welfare officer came later that day to tell her that her husband had been incarcerated, leaving her with two small dependent children and no money. I was disgusted. Then a pathetic-looking man stood and shamefully admitted that he had once wet himself sitting at the roulette table because he could not tear himself away, being totally convinced that his number was going to come up. Even the warm, odorous liquid trickling down his leg could

not compel him to save his dignity and leave. Demeaning confessionals followed, each person proudly stating how many years they had been free of the curse of gambling, thanks to GA.

Then Richard stood. He looked sad and embarrassed, a barely recognisable image of the man I had married. His voice was weak, and it was hard to follow what he was saying.

'My name is Richard, and I am a compulsive gambler. I have been lying to my wife for years about the extent of my gambling and I have now run out of options.'

I looked at him as he rambled on and didn't see the handsome man I had married; just a sad shadow of the person for whom I had now lost all respect.

'I've forged my wife's signatures on life insurance documents, I've lost my job as a solicitor, and I'm currently being investigated for misappropriation of funds. I am awaiting trial and...' Here he faltered and he swallowed deeply. 'I may well go to prison.'

It was even worse than Richard had admitted to me, and I was drowning. I loathed him for being so weak that he could only admit to the full and ugly extent of what he had done with the security of a group of strangers around him. I sat there disgusted and devastated. The one thing I knew for sure was that this was certainly not a community that I wanted to be part of.

The anger raging inside of me was so intense that I had to leave. I walked out of the hall, hailed the nearest taxi and cried throughout the long journey across London. I childishly hoped that when he finally left the meeting, he would run out of petrol. He was definitely bringing out the absolute worst in me.

Suddenly, all those murmured 'work' calls made sense. He had been trying to stave off the debtors who were demanding their money back. All I knew was that I would arrange to see a lawyer and work out my options for taking you, Edna, with me. Days earlier, I decided that I could not deny Richard his daughter, but now it was completely different. One thing was for sure; I could leave him, but not you, so I needed to see what my options were and then formulate a plan.

⤦

Unable to tear herself away, although hating what she was reading, Edna felt compelled to carry on. Her mind was racing and her head pounding as she continued to absorb what her mother had lived through. She missed lunch, a hitherto unheard-of happening, and continued to read.

⤦

Feeling more optimistic than I had in weeks, I called Bill and told him the news that actually meant that all was not yet lost for us.

'Darling, see the very best lawyer you can because I don't care what it costs. This is our future that we are talking about.'

Feeling more optimistic than I had in months, I called my friend Suzanne, who had just been through a very ugly divorce yet had come out smiling the other side, and asked if she could recommend her solicitor for a cousin of mine. I telephoned the number she gave me and managed to get an after-hours appointment for the following week. It was a very long week, and I could hardly concentrate on anything, waiting to hear whether I still had a life or not.

Finally, the appointed day arrived. The taxi stopped at a most imposing and beautiful Georgian house in Mayfair. I walked up to the front door and pressed the bell, and I was ushered into a grand reception area.

A mouse-like young woman greeted me and informed me in a girly, breathy voice that her name was Camilla. 'Miss Fostrup will see you now.' She led me along the corridor, chatting about nothing that I can remember. I just wished she would keep quiet and leave me with my thoughts. Finally, she stopped at a heavily polished mahogany door and her incessant chatter abated. She knocked three times, and a voice announced:

'Come.'

My heart was pounding as the mouse opened the door. The 'lioness' stood as I entered and shook my hand, gesturing me to sit on the opposite side of her Art Deco desk. She was a very glamorous woman, with a shock of perfectly coiffed jet-black hair, immaculately dressed in what I recognised was a beautifully-cut Balmain suit. Her long lithe legs, peeping out from a pencil skirt, were held steady by a perfectly formed pair of black court shoes. I felt that I was in the presence of greatness. She was charming but firm, explaining that my life was to be condensed into a one-hour consultation. She warned that my replies to her questions should be kept brief, as the clock on her not inconsequential hourly fee would be racking up fast. Finally, after considering all the facts, she dealt a bitter blow.

'I am afraid that the finances are easy to deal with, but as to your daughter, there is no way that you can take her to live outside the UK without the permission of her father.'

I was crushed, knowing full well that it was not going to happen. Richard would never agree to that. To my utter dismay, I realised that if I could not take you out of the country, and Bill couldn't stay in London because of his responsibility to his dependent wife, there was no future for us. I wasn't even sure that you would agree anyway, even with the lure of fun and excitement of New York. I decided that Bill needed another chance to find happiness, and as for me, I was trapped and broken, never to be mended.

I left the offices a lot less confident than I had been when I had entered and called Bill to tell him the bad news.

'Don't be rash, darling, let me work something out,' Bill begged me.

'There is nothing to work out,' I said miserably. 'I can't leave my daughter, and you can't leave your wife. There is no way that we can make this work.'

✍

Edna felt so guilty because she knew that at that moment in time, her mother had been right, and there was no way she would have left her adored daddy. She had to acknowledge that, without realising it before, she was the reason for her mother's unhappiness. Iris would have been happy if she could have pursued her life with Bill, and the dreadful truth that Iris's life would not have ended the way it did was too much for Edna to bear. There were no biscuits for Edna today!

✍

15*th* September 1966

Deciding that another restaurant meal would make not a blind bit of difference to our finances, Richard asked me out for dinner so that we could talk in private. We made our menu selection without discussion, me a simple salad and Richard the T-bone steak medium rare with well-done chips, fried onions and sautéed mushrooms, all of which were ordered directly to the bored waiter without deference to each other. It struck me as extraordinary that, even after being caught with his hand in the cookie jar, his appetite had not been affected in the slightest. Looking at the other tables all engaged in animated conversation, glasses tinkling and candles burning, I was heartbroken that all we had to talk about was the dismal state of our marriage and the even more wretched state of our finances. It was clear that we would not have enough money to run two homes, and so I reluctantly gave in and decided to stay in what for me was now a totally loveless marriage. I was devastated that Bill and I could no longer pursue our dream, and I resented Richard bitterly for it.

The one thing upon which we were both in agreement was that you,

Edna, should not suffer, so, knowing that leaving him and taking you with me was hopeless, I agreed to stay with him for your sake, but I told him that it was only until the outcome of the court case. I made it clear that if he were to go to prison there would be no point in me sitting at home waiting for him.

That night I called Bill to tell him that there was no us anymore.

Bill got on the next flight to London, trying to change my mind, but it was hopeless. We were sitting on a bench in Richmond Park, and no one dared come near upon hearing my heart-wrenching sobs. I was inconsolable, and Bill very wisely waited until I was spent before he spoke. As much as he tried to talk me out of it, I knew that there was no future for us. Much as I loved him, I could not and would not leave you, Edna. My duty as a mother came above all else, and I had to put your happiness above mine.

There was no way I could go home looking and sounding so terrible. Eventually, when I could cry no longer, I just sat there numb and uncommunicative. Poor Bill. He tried to put his arms around me, but I just pushed him away cruelly. For me, if there was no hope for us, there was no point in continuing. Better to get it over quickly and not drag out the inevitable. I just wanted to go home and forget that we had ever met. After assuring him that I could drive, I let him see me to my car, and I shall never forget the sight of him in my rear window. The handsome, confident man that I had fallen in love with just looked frail and old as he disappeared out of sight.

Slowly I made the journey home, punishing myself by listening to Frank Sinatra singing 'In the wee small hours of the morning'. I wanted to get the crying over before I got home, but it wasn't working, and the tempestuous sea of tears raging inside of me showed no sign of receding. I let myself into the house and told you that I thought I was coming down with a bug and would sleep in the spare room. Once alone, I threw myself on the bed and sobbed into my pillow.

28th September 1966

I stopped eating and my rages, hysteria and melancholy became worse and worse as the days went on. I couldn't even muster the strength to hide it from you. I am filled with shame that my inability to cope with life overshadowed my responsibility to your needs, Edna, putting mine before yours.

Richard took me to see a psychiatrist who wanted me immediately admitted to hospital, and I just followed instructions and allowed myself the selfish extravagance of a nervous breakdown despite my thirteen-year-old daughter needing me at home. If I couldn't have Bill I just didn't want to exist. This was a period in my life that I am not proud of.

As Edna read this, she was shaking with shock and guilt. She remembered how all she had been concerned with at the tender age of thirteen was how her special birthday had been a washout, with her mother crying all the time, whereas all Edna had wanted to do was to have fun with her best friend Daisy and dream about Michael Eden. Now a mature woman nearly 70 years of age, she asked herself how she could have been so self-obsessed. She had blamed her mother for so many years and now, through her mother's confessions, she saw the wretchedness of Iris's life in blazing technicolour, but she still could not get her head around her own mother having had an affair. Edna was far more of a prude than she had realised.

By now starving hungry, Edna decided to order in. She called Mario's Pizzas and ordered what he described as 'the whole works'. Cheese, tomato, artichokes, mushrooms, onions and salami. Twenty minutes later she was tucking in with relish and actually managed to eat the whole thing!

She knew that she owed it to her late mother to see what other information she could uncover, and although Richard was now in a nursing home in a haze of dementia, he was the only person left who knew what had happened. Even though she couldn't ask him, she decided that tomorrow she would go and visit him. Who knew what secrets might lie there within his pathetic belongings?

Mentally exhausted, she made her way up to bed carrying her precious book, together with two carefully wrapped custard creams. Edna wanted to carry on with the story and again turned the pages. Her mother's familiar script was speaking to her again as she read the entry detailing Richard's downfall.

❧

26th February 1967

After a long six-month wait, Richard finally went to court today. Unluckily for him, the judge decided that he would benefit from two years in an open prison. Edna, you are devastated, Richard is downtrodden and broken, and I am desolate that it has all come too late for my life with Bill. I just can't believe that this man who pervaded my very being accepted the situation and didn't even try to contact me, let alone try to change my mind. I'm still so sad that he didn't fight for me. I read him so wrongly. I really thought I was the love of his life. He was certainly mine, but there is no point letting him know that I am now free. I've just got to move on and make a new life for myself.

Even with what he has done, Richard is still your father, and it is only natural that you still adore him. As I warned him I would, I am now going to instigate divorce proceedings. He doesn't have the money to fight me, so I hope that this will be quick and relatively painless. Divorce can never be easy because no one goes into a marriage thinking that it will end, but hopefully this will not be acrimonious, and we can both move forward with our lives. Despite all that Richard has done, I still bear him no ill will and genuinely hope he can find happiness after this dreadful time is over.

❧

Edna turned the pages, blinking back the tears as she continued reading her mother's painful words. As they danced across the page, she decided that she couldn't continue to read any more; it was too emotionally draining, and she carefully closed the book again.

Within moments sleep took over and she was running. Running so fast that she fell into a bottomless pit and awoke soaking wet. She showered quickly, selected a clean nightie and was soon sleeping peacefully.

Chapter Four

Friday

EDNA ROSE EARLY. Sleep was eluding her these days and she just longed to return to normality. She went downstairs and prepared a lazy breakfast of a jam sandwich and a cup of tea as she was totally preoccupied with preparing for her appointment at the bank. After rushing upstairs for a quick bath, she dressed in the first thing that poked out at her from the wardrobe. Having no intention of staying long enough to take her coat off, she didn't really care what she wore. She went downstairs again, opened the drawer of the hall table and, despite it being a rainy day, removed a pair of sunglasses, and then reached above to the hat stand to take her floppy rain hat. She looked in the mirror and was quite pleased with what she saw. *I doubt even my mother would know me now.* She hobbled down to the bank with her very strange and recognisable gait. Standing outside, her heart pounding, she took a deep breath, popped one of her 'calming down' pills and furtively entered. She made her way over to the desk where a rather rotund woman with pink cheeks sat. *She's clearly had too many apple pies!* Edna mused.

The bored-looking woman was peering down at a book on her lap while trying to pretend that she was busy.

'I have an appointment at half past twelve to close my account,' Edna said in an unusually quiet voice. The last thing she wanted was to draw attention to herself. Heaven forbid that Franklyn would come out of his office and notice her, but he was already waiting for her.

'Good morning, Mrs Watson, please come in,' he gushed. The man wore a navy single-breasted suit which was pulling across his burgeoning stomach, and a pink self-patterned shirt set off with a blue and pink polyester tie. She noticed that his shoes were polished and his socks an acceptable shade of dark navy. He had ruddy cheeks and an incredibly crimson nose. *No doubt the product of an excess of alcohol, particularly the red sort.* Edna's high and mighty attitude was in full flow. Yet for all her bravado, she could feel the colour flushing through her body; and it wasn't the usual fire.

'I'm in a terrible hurry and I just want to sign the forms.'

'Of course you do, just come this way.'

She resisted the arm that was trying to usher her into his office.

'I do not take kindly to being manhandled, so take your hand off me now!' she yelled at him.

'Now, now, Mrs Watson, let's not frighten everyone. If you would just step inside my office, you could sign the forms, I could witness them, and you could be on your way.'

Edna went limp and let him lead her into his office, a totally nondescript and anonymous room with a 1970s G Plan teak desk and black revolving chair.

'So tell me, Mrs Watson,' he purred in his most friendly voice. 'Why do you want to close your account? We here at FNC really value your custom and I, as your bank manager, would like to offer my services as your trusted advisor. I could go through your finances with you and show you where you could make savings, ensuring that you would have enough capital to see you through to the end of your days.'

'It's none of your business. None of it is,' she said through gritted teeth. 'Now give me the forms. I'm in a hurry.'

Edna noticed that Franklyn was perspiring profusely.

'If you will just sign here, where I have placed a cross, add your name and address and, of course,' Edna saw him stifle a snigger, 'the reason for closing your account.'

Edna filled in the required information as quickly as her hand would allow and when it came to the reason for leaving, she wrote in very definite script: *I don't like the dog anymore!* She slammed her chequebook and card on the table and exited with Catherine wheels and rockets going off in her chest.

Still shaken by the confrontation at the bank and now late for lunch, Edna felt her stomach begin to grumble as she hurriedly made her way home. As soon as she arrived, still smarting from the unfortunate episode with the bank manager, she poured herself a 'medicinal' brandy to steady her nerves. Annoyed with herself for not leaving even one single slice of pizza last night to soothe her angry stomach, she made herself a banana sandwich.

Having read about her mother's trip to New York, Edna decided that after this unsettling period in her life was over, she deserved a holiday. She had always enjoyed the travel as much as the holiday, and it had been far too long. Don had taken her to some amazing places over the years. Thailand, Vietnam, India, central America, South America, The Fjords in Norway and Sweden, France, Italy, the list just went on and on. She mused about how the terminal at Heathrow Airport had always been a place of great excitement and wonder to her, starting with their incredible honeymoon all those years ago. The airport was the signal that she was about to embark on an adventure. What did it signal for other people? she wondered. So many endless possibilities and Edna had loved trying to guess why they were travelling. A visit to much missed family, a trip to a desert island. The fervent hope of a successful business deal. All around, everyone always focused on their own mission.

The last time that Edna had travelled was on a celebratory birthday trip to Paris with the girls. She had been shocked at all the hubbub, dazzling lighting, and duty-free shops tempting people to eat, drink, dress and make up… each to an excess. The sound of sales pitches from heavily made-up assistants urging naïve customers to buy, buy, and buy. The staff sitting behind desks. Some with a cheerful smile. Some with an 'I've been on this shift for eleven hours, just watching the clock to home time' tired and bored look. Airline crews pulling along their cabin bags with an authoritative stride. Some giggling about what happened last night. Some wondering if their IVF treatment was going to work and hopefully only an odd (G-d forbid) flight crew hoping that last night's drinking binge would not be discovered in a random check. Then there were the main characters in the scene. The travellers. Some looking like the cast of *The Only Way is Essex* with their designer sunglasses, large Stetson hats and equally large lips. Lone, tired and frustrated mothers trying to deal with fretful babies that won't settle whilst simultaneously trying to control a six-year-old boy pulling gooner faces at a lady in a wheelchair. Then there were the newly-weds starting their honeymoon right there in full view of everyone, and the business traveller with an open-collared white shirt, black trousers and obligatory earpiece, looking like Kevin Costner in *The Bodyguard*. No, she concluded that travel was not the luxury experience, reserved only for the privileged, that it once was. No doubt about it, if she wanted to go on another trip, she was certainly going to have to brace herself!

She moved into the sitting room and started to read again, but she was just unable to concentrate.

❧

As soon as Edna had left, Franklyn started trembling. He knew that he would be in trouble at Trident and his source of feeding Margaret's pleasure would come to an untimely end if he could not accomplish his mission. Even worse was the prospect of his wife finding out what he had been up to.

Reluctantly, he called Edward Clitheroe to relay the news that Edna Watson had closed her account.

'Hello, Franklyn here. I can't get anywhere with Edna Watson, and regrettably, I'm out.'

'Oh no, you don't get off so easily, my man. We're in it for the long haul. Reg won't accept your resignation and if you defy him, we'll make sure your little wife knows all about your "other" life.' The line went dead.

Franklyn knew what he had to do, starting with Margaret. He picked up the receiver and dialled her number.

'Are you free tonight?'

'Always for you, big boy.'

Two hours later, sitting in her boudoir, which was the only way to describe her tasteless and over-the-top bedroom, the rather common woman with over-bleached blonde hair and over-botoxed pouting lips was screaming shrilly at him.

'What do you mean, it's over? I say when it's over, not you. Do you want me to tell your wife exactly what her snivelling little husband has been up to?'

'Margaret, please be reasonable. I could go to prison. We have to stop seeing each other, at least until things die down.' He was beginning to retreat, coward that he was.

'I don't care if you go to prison! Do you honestly think that I was really interested in you! You sorry creature. I was only in it for what I could get. You disgust me with your milk-white wrinkly skin and paunchy stomach. How could you ever have thought that I could be interested in someone like you?'

He suddenly realised how stupid he had been. *She's right. Why would an attractive and sexy young woman like Margaret have been interested in me? All I was to her was another Gucci handbag!*

He put his head in his hands, feeling his bald patches as if for the first time, and realised he had thrown his life away on a whim for some little bitch, but he acknowledged that he had only himself to blame. His ill-conceived conception of their relationship, as well as the lower part of his anatomy, had overruled what had once been quite an astute brain.

'Out you go,' she said callously.

Completely dejected and downtrodden, he slunk out of her flat and made his way down the steep staircase. It occurred to him that it might be easier if he just fell down the stairs, but he recognised that the fall might not kill him, possibly just leave him permanently incapacitated. That, he concluded, would be an even bigger mess. He decided to go back to the office to call Edward and tell him it was over, which was not going to be pleasant either.

'I don't want to be disturbed,' he whispered to the receptionist without even acknowledging her. 'Please cancel my appointments. I won't be taking calls for the rest of the afternoon.' With shaking hands, he called the Trident offices. He was hot and sweaty; his heart was pumping overtime, and he was desperately trying to find a way out. But there was no way out. He had messed up big time.

'Toby Franklyn for Edward Clitheroe.'

'Just a moment, Mr Franklyn, while I find him for you.'

Franklyn stared into space, looking for inspiration when he knew that there was none to be found.

'Toby, my boy have you seen sense? Tell me that I can sleep easy tonight.'

'Well, the thing is…'

'Now, don't you go telling me that you can't do it. That would be an extremely stupid thing to do, don't you think?'

Franklyn swallowed hard. This was not going to be easy. Either way he was going to be trussed up like a turkey. 'The thing is,' he continued, 'rather like the formidable Mrs Thatcher, the lady's not for turning, and I just don't know what to do.'

'Well, you'd better come up with something because Reg doesn't like being disappointed.'

The line went dead, and Franklyn was left staring at the receiver as if he had never seen one before.

Clitheroe, in turn, called his boss, Reg Hopkins, a short, tubby man with saveloy fingers to match.

'She's proving to be quite a handful. Franklyn just called to say she's closed her account.'

'I see. Well, it's time to call in pest control, isn't it! Get Benny.' And the older voice gave a wicked laugh. Reg Hopkins acknowledged that if he wanted to get the house, it was going to take drastic measures, and Benny the Brick was the one to do it. Benny was a very faithful 'heavy' from his father's days in the East End. He was called 'Benny the Brick' because his body was rumoured to be impenetrable.

Edward Clitheroe dialled again.

''Allo,' a rough and common voice answered.

'Hello, Benny. It's Edward Clitheroe. Reg has got a little job for you. Very urgent. A stupid woman has turned down our offer to buy her house. She won't budge and she's holding up our whole scheme. Can you get pest control organised?'

'Don't you worry yourself. Just give me 'er address and you tell Mr H, we'll give 'er a good shakin' up,' the coarse voice reassured the frustrated man.

Edna had unbelievably missed her afternoon biscuits, not having been able to tear herself away from the book, but it was now six o'clock and she was feeling decidedly hungry. She opened the freezer, looking for the quickest and easiest solution to her malnourishment, and there poking out from behind the Wall's Viennetta was a chicken and leek pie with mash. Just for good measure she hacked off a piece of the ice cream and put the remains (such as they were) back in the freezer. She didn't hear the letterbox receiving a delivery.

Edna moved into the sitting room and was remembering how, during her mother's depression, she was sent in each morning to give her mother a dutiful kiss before going to school and then again when she got home. After repeating the process, she would go into her room, turn on her music to full blast and sulk.

Even at thirteen years of age she could see that her father was at his wits' end, and she tried to eavesdrop whenever she could to find out what was going on. She heard her father ask their doctor for advice. The doctor referred Iris to a psychiatrist, who persuaded Richard that she needed hospitalisation.

Edna had insisted on going to the appointment and could still remember the conversation verbatim, almost as if it were yesterday.

'This is a really extreme case, and we need to give her mind a rest. I am proposing to give your wife a revolutionary new sleep treatment called Narcosis. She will not be distressed or uncomfortable. She will just lie there sleeping whilst we observe her. We will feed her intravenously and attend to all her needs. I am hoping that after giving her brain a break from her trauma, this treatment will give her the strength to accept the situation and move on when we wake her.'

'I have no choice but to agree,' Richard said sadly. 'I have to put my trust in you.'

'Do you have medical insurance?'

'Yes, yes, thankfully I do.'

'Well, let's get on with it without delay.'

Edna quickly moved away from the door.

Arrangements were immediately made, and Iris was transferred the next day to a private nursing home in Regent's Park. She lay there, to all intents and purposes, looking very peaceful and fast asleep. For three interminable weeks Edna would just go and stare at her mother. Of course, Edna knew her father didn't want her to see Iris like that, but she was and always had been strong-willed, and she had insisted.

During that time, whilst Iris was lying in the nursing home, there was a big family party planned at the Dorchester Hotel in London and it was decided that it would do Edna good if she and Richard attended, even for a short while, just to have a break. It was going to be a fantastic and most extravagant party, and Edna was so excited to be her father's escort. Daisy had just been to her sister's wedding and loaned Edna the most beautiful dress. It was sleeveless with a hot pink silk organza bodice and shoestring straps. The A-line skirt was made of silk taffeta and the silver court shoes completed the look. Edna had never felt so good.

She was nervous when she stepped into the room and, overwhelmed with the scene in front of her, she grabbed her father's arm tightly. She had never experienced anything like it. The walls were decorated with antique mirrors, and the flower arrangements looked as high as the sky. Champagne was served in what Edna learned were called coup glasses, but of course, she was not allowed to taste it. However, she was given a Shirley Temple, which was a blend of lemonade and grenadine served exactly like a champagne cocktail. Tiny morsels of food were being passed around, and she couldn't take her eyes off the little delectable bites of smoked salmon on rounds of toast, chopped chicken liver pâté in weeny pastry cups and minuscule mushroom vol-au-vents. Edna's eyes were darting around the room, and having worked out where the food was appearing from, she became fixated on the service doors to see when and where the next delicious delicacies would appear. She was absolutely ravenous and couldn't eat enough of them.

They were called to dinner, and Edna was relieved to be sitting at a family table next to her father. She was also comforted to find that she was not seated next to her Aunt and Uncle. Thankfully they were a few seats away, out of her line of vision. Similarly, she had been dreading being seated with a group of youngsters her age. She had it in her mind that they would all know each other and would exclude her from the conversation. Luckily, Richard had a word in the right ear and the problem was sorted. He discreetly whispered in her ear, telling her which cutlery to use, as he had seen her horror when confronted with so many knives and forks. The first course to be served was fresh asparagus flown in from California. Again, Edna was confused as to how to eat it, but she just followed her father's lead. The main course was called boeuf en croute, which she discovered was roast beef sitting on chopped mushrooms encased in pastry. The Hereford beef was succulent and delicious, and by now a far more relaxed Edna was having a whale of a time, savouring all these new delights. The potatoes were mouth-watering, having been whipped and piped like little meringue peaks. The dessert came in held high on silver trays with spun sugar that looked just like a bird's nest. Some people were joking that it looked like Ethel Rogers' hair. Ethel was the local gossip who used to have her hair dressed in a similar style with so much hair lacquer that it didn't move. When she got to the hairdresser every week, it took two juniors to disman-tle it before washing and restyling again. In the good old days, Edna had loved going to the hairdresser with her mother just to watch.

There followed a very dramatic moment in the evening when Ethel approached the top table, leaned over the candelabra to com-pliment the hostess on the magnificent party, desperately trying to find out the name of the caterer and florist. Not that Ethel had any intention of using their services but, being inherently nosy, she just wanted to find out what everything cost. Within moments, Ethel's hair was on fire and two quick-thinking men jumped up to run to her aid. One was beating her hair with napkins whilst the other doused her with a jug of ice-cold water. Ethel was carried off crying and had to be taken home.

Upon remembering this, Edna chuckled. Although the memory of Iris lying in hospital whilst she was having such a good time made her sad, she still couldn't help laughing at poor old Ethel.

Iris was no better after the planned treatment, so Richard was summoned to the hospital for a meeting with the psychiatrist. Edna insisted on accompanying him as she wanted to know what was going to happen with her mother. She watched the dapper man in his blue pinstripe suit, white shirt and army tie as he smoked with his rather exaggerated plumes of smoke filling the room.

'I'm afraid that subconsciously your wife is rather enjoying her time here. I think she is far too comfortable in a private facility, and I want to move her to a National Health hospital, which I hope will scare her into getting better.'

Studying the two men, not wanting to miss a word of the conversation, Edna could tell that Richard intensely disliked the pompous man, but she could also see that her father was clutching at straws, and so he agreed to the doctor's advice. The following day Iris was transferred by ambulance to the hospital in Lambeth, and after two days of a strict 'no visitors' policy to allow her to settle in, Edna and Richard walked into the grey and forbidding building. Edna was nervously clutching her father's hand, her nails stabbing him to the point at which they might draw blood. As they walked into the ward, they saw the bars on the windows and Edna felt nauseous at the sickly and overbearing smell of antiseptic. The metal bed frames were lined up on either side of the ward with the nurses' desks in the middle. There was a woman screaming that the

Nazis were coming to get her, and a lot of moaning and crying emanated from the other patients. It was terrifying and the closest thing to a mental institution that Edna was ever likely to see. It was one thing to see her mother lying in bed fast asleep in a private room in Regent's Park, but quite another to see her in this horrific environment. Edna was sure that as long as she lived, she would be haunted by the horrific scene that no one, let alone a thirteen-year-old, should witness. After so many years, Edna still doubted that she would ever be able to erase it completely from her mind. As much as she wanted to see her mother, Edna was so scared and wanted to run away, desperately wanting Iris to stop this and return to being a mother. She loved her mother dearly, but at the same time she resented her for allowing herself the luxury of a breakdown. What about her mother's responsibility to her and to her Daddy? Now with the reality of how unpleasant the experience actually was, Edna was not in such a hurry to continue these visits and for the rest of Iris's stay there, Edna left Richard to go alone.

After two weeks, and to the relief of everyone, Iris finally complained that she hated it there and wanted to be taken home. This was a good sign, and what they had all been waiting for. Once home, things pretty much returned to normal, or as least as normal as it was ever going to be with a mother who was highly strung, had lost the love of her life, and was left saddled with a useless husband who had blown their life savings.

Years later, Edna realised that Iris's breakdown had probably been coming for years. Her mother had finally succumbed to this state of mind, causing Edna's progress into the wide world to degrade even further. Excelling at Maths and English and a painfully shy teenager, Edna was inept socially, and observed rather than joined in. She had longed for a mother like Daisy's, who would bake biscuits and invite her friends around for tea, but that was not to be.

Thinking about biscuits, Edna raided the biscuit jar, wrapped two chocolate digestives in a paper napkin and carried them, along with her precious book, upstairs.

Munching away, she started to read, but her eyes just would not focus, and she decided to call it a night, so after sweeping away the crumbs, which, despite her good intentions, had managed to fall onto the sheets, within moments she was fast asleep. She was soon awakened by a scratching noise. Sitting bolt upright in bed, she turned on the bedside lamp and there, scurrying across the bedroom floor, was a grey indistinct something. She couldn't make out what it was; it moved so quickly. She rubbed her eyes twice and looked again. There, darting in the opposite direction, was a mouse – at least she hoped it was a mouse. Edna got up, mustering every bit of her courage, went downstairs and fetched a garden broom and a pair of rubber gloves. She entered the bedroom gingerly and danced around the room, whacking the terrified animal every time she saw it.

Eventually she stunned the creature, and bravely holding it between her Marigolds, trying to focus on the stairs, instead of the offending body in her hands, she made her way carefully down to the front door, walked out into the garden and deposited it in the now redundant wishing well before trundling back to bed.

CHAPTER FIVE

Saturday

EDNA AROSE IN quite an anxious state. She was still shaken by the week's events and by last night's unwelcome visitor, and extremely agitated about Olivia and Viola's impending visit. She had still not decided whether or not to unburden herself to them.

Not considering herself the best of mothers in the way that she dealt with things, she didn't want to get it wrong again. She particularly remembered when Olivia's marriage had broken down, and she had to finally acknowledge that she had not been much help. She felt ashamed as she vividly recalled how her daughter had confided in her and how her reaction to the news must have seemed so uncaring.

'Mother, Joe has left me,' Olivia sobbed down the phone. 'I can't believe what he's done. He suggested that we go for a walk on the beach. Things hadn't been great, as you know, so I saw this as a sign that he wanted to get things back on track. Of course, I wanted to look good, so I slipped into my favourite powder-blue jeans and a crisp white shirt, collar turned up and hem just below the thigh. A pair of pale blue moccasins completed the stylish but 'just thrown together' look as I wanted to appear very casual. I ran my fingers through my hair and took one last approving look in the mirror and I was pretty OK with what I saw.'

At this point, Edna was wondering why, at such a monumental point in her life, when Olivia was about to impart the details of such a serious event, her self-obsessed daughter was prattling on about her appearance.

'We hardly spoke in the car,' Olivia went on. 'With me trying to make trivial conversation that elicited absolutely no response. I commented on the tree damage, the houses on the new development, Angela's new au pair... all to no avail. We arrived at the beach, and he stared at the sand, looking like a boy whose mother had just found his porno magazine stash. '

'I'm going back to Marilyn.' He just blurted it out, mumbling this devastating news into the tiny grains of sand that were once the scene of so many of our happy family barbecues.

'I tell you, Mother, if he had hit me in the chest with the full force of his honed body, courtesy of the So Alive gym, he could not have wounded me more. So, my husband, with whom I had just celebrated twenty years of wedded...what? Certainly not bliss...was going back to his first wife after all these years. He said that for him, there had been more bad than good in our marriage, so there was just no point in continuing.' Olivia went on and on, hardly stopping for breath. 'It appears that five months ago he went to his old house to help with his daughter's homework. You know, that anorexic girl with the ring through her nose? When he'd finished the abstract algebra – and you know how good he is at maths, City traders always are, aren't they? – his sixteen-year-old daughter thanked him and announced that she was off to her friend's house for a sleepover. He said that before he and Marilyn knew it, one glass of wine led to another, and they started talking about how much they missed the easy banter. He then went on in graphic detail. Can you believe that he could be so cruel? Mother, you know how impetuous he's always been, and evidently the stupid man thought Marilyn looked so gorgeous, in what was I am sure a very carefully chosen satin top with just the right amount of décolletage, accompanied by that familiar waft of Chanel No 5, that, surprise, surprise, he once again found her absolutely irresistible. Obviously Marilyn had manoeuvred the whole thing!' Olivia started snivelling again.

Edna had not been able to help smiling wryly at the thought that *it takes one to know one.*

'Meanwhile,' Olivia prattled on, 'I'm sure that at that mad heady point, it never occurred to either of them that what was wrong twenty-five years ago would probably raise its ugly head again before long, but I don't have enough time for them to get to that point. I felt as if he had physically wounded me, and in fact I still do. Anyway, totally unprepared for this shocking revelation, I heard this well-controlled robot (which I didn't recognise was me) utter, "I'll be back in a moment," as I walked away back down the deserted part of the beach, unkempt, full of flotsam and jetsam, where I could scream to my heart's content without fear of anyone rushing to my aid. When I was done, empty and depleted, I walked back up the beach and found him kicking shells into the surf. I asked him for the car keys, telling him that I had forgotten something. Do you know that he didn't even ask me what I needed? He handed them over and so, grabbing them tightly, I walked slowly and deliberately back up to the road to the car. I started the ignition and without a second glance drove back to London. I just wanted to cause him pain and punish him for what he had put me through. As I drove the long, miserable journey home, I didn't once wonder how he would get back. Oh, Mother, what am I going to do?'

Edna, to her abject shame, had merely asked Olivia whether she had let things slip in the bedroom.

Now, this morning, despite having told her daughters that she was considering not attending the funeral, Edna was beginning to waver, terrified at having to face her aunt and confront her with what she and her husband had done all those years ago, but at the same time, wanting to grab the opportunity to put the whole ugly business to rest. The truth was that if she went through with it, and that was an extremely big if, she really didn't know whether it would make her feel better or worse. She didn't think that she wanted to tell her daughters her reason for not wanting to go because she felt that this was something private to her and not for sharing with them.

'Oh, what to do, what to do. What do you think, Don?' Again, Edna was downhearted by the silence. 'How could you have left me on my own to deal with everything? You were supposed to look after me and instead you deserted me.' At this she started crying, deep racking sobs. 'Oh, forgive me, my love. I take it all back. I didn't mean it. It's just that I am so lonely without you, and after twenty years, I still can't get used to it.'

Edna just kept moving backwards and forwards on her thoughts about attending the funeral. There was only one thing for it. She gave her nose a loud blow. *Yes, something to take my mind off everything. Breakfast!* The indecision was exhausting. Stomach rumbling, Edna quickly set about preparing some nourishment. After finishing her well-toasted sourdough with thickly spread strawberry jam, completing the *Times* crossword and smashing the *Daily Mail* Sudoku, she went upstairs for her bath. Over and over she wrestled with her thoughts and yet again the Youth Dew was failing to work its magic. There was just too much going on in her head.

Having spent far too long reflecting, Edna looked at her wrist-watch, which she had placed carefully at the side of the bath, collected her thoughts, and shivered as the water had now become cold. Reaching for the towel and placing it around her shoulders, she walked into the bedroom. She studied the bedframe and ran her fingers lovingly around it. This place that she had leaned against whilst she and Don had joined as one. This place where Don had propped a pillow against whilst reading in bed. This place where she had nursed her babies, full of promise of the future ahead. This place where she had slept alone for the first time since she and Don were married. These thoughts were Edna at her gentlest and most vulnerable.

⤸

She dressed quickly so that she would not be late for her daughters' bi-monthly visit and made her way downstairs. Sitting at the kitchen table to wait for them, Edna turned her attention back to the funeral. Unfortunately, within moments her thoughts were disturbed when the doorbell rang and, thinking it was the girls, Edna made her way to the door. She was shocked to find Edward Clitheroe standing there, with a sickly half-grin on his face, revealing his yellowed teeth and sending his halitosis hurtling across the threshold. The most unwelcome and uninvited visitor asked if he could come in. Edna was so shocked at his lack of manners (*I mean, who turns up without asking?*) that she found herself ushering him into the hallway but definitely not inviting him into the sitting room. She gave him another of her steely looks, whereupon, full of nerves, he again vastly overplayed his hand.

'Hello, Mrs Watson. I'm so sorry to disturb you unannounced, but I was just wondering whether you had had any more thoughts about my offer. My wife is driving me crazy because she so wants the house.'

'How dare you turn up without an appointment? Do you not understand the Queen's English? I am *not* moving, so be off with you!'

'I urge you to think about this seriously, Mrs Watson. My wife has asked me to increase our offer to one million pounds. How does that sound?'

'If you don't leave my premises, I shall call the police and report you for trespassing.'

Unable to stop, and now in full flow, Edward bumbled on. 'I mean, it's a big house to take care of on your own, and quite isolated in terms of potential unwanted visitors, be they human or of the rodent kind, if you follow my drift. A good friend of mine mentioned that there has been a scourge of unwelcome visitors, and I was thinking that you might be having trouble in that department. Heh, heh, heh.'

Edna, perceptive as ever, now realised what the incident with the mouse last night had been about. Giving him her coldest and most determined look, she launched at him and, without so much as a by your leave, picked up the broom that was still at the front door and rapped poor Mr Clitheroe extremely strongly across the knuckles, causing blood to trickle from his hand. Stunned by her attack, he let out a hideous scream, as much from shock as from pain, and ran up the drive crying.

Now she knew for sure that Edward Clitheroe was up to something, but what? She was going to have to do some serious digging to find out what the ghastly man was up to.

'And don't bother to cross my door again,' she yelled after him. 'If you ever think of sending me unwanted gifts again, you will be looking at the eagle eye of the magistrate if I have anything to do with it. Now be off with you and thank your lucky stars that this time it was just a warning!'

At the same time, a bemused Olivia and Viola were arriving. Olivia, the tall and lanky clothes horse looking like the latest edition of *Vogue*, and Viola, pretty and unassuming in her Boden blue print midi dress.

'Who was that?' they sang in unison.

'Nobody that should concern you. Don't just stand there letting the cold in. Quickly then, into the kitchen.'

Edna studied her daughters. Both lovely, but so different. Olivia had an almost Middle Eastern look, with her dark, straight hair and large almond-shaped eyes. Her eyebrows were thick and lustrous, her eyelashes full and long. By contrast, Viola was petite and feminine with blonde, curly hair and blue eyes. Olivia was materialistic and always on the lookout for a rich man to help fund her lavish lifestyle, whereas Viola was very bright and extremely happy with her family and sprawling home set in loads of acres in the middle of nowhere.

'Why do I always get the feeling that there's a slice of your life of which we know nothing at all?' said Olivia.

'And why do you, Miss Busybody, have to be so nosy? Why must people go poking into places that don't concern them? Instead of standing there admiring your reflection in the kettle, why don't you get on with making the tea?'

'Mother, you're exasperating. I am not "people", and I'm merely asking why you feel the need to go to Uncle Harold's funeral, the prospect of which is clearly upsetting you. Does your dislike of him have something to do with your reluctance to tell us about the secret that we know you're keeping? Why do you feel the need to keep things from Viola and me? Maybe we could help if you'd talk about it.'

'Because some things are better left hidden and no good can come of disturbing a den of snakes. Can't you see that you are upsetting me? Can't you see that I have no wish to rake up the past?' *A past that makes me feel full of panic and revulsion at the very reminder of something that happened so many years ago.* 'Please, just let it be.'

'Did you discuss it with Father? Did he know?' Viola, the kindest of the two sisters, dared to ask.

Of course, my Don, Edna thought wistfully.

'Yes, he and my doll Peggy were the only ones I've ever told. Oh, aside from the crackpot counsellor that your father dragged me to,' Edna continued. 'A brown rice sandal merchant to boot.

You know the type. The mere idea of me sitting cross-legged on the floor singing Kumbaya had me reaching for the Ketel One vodka. Anyway, even if I managed to get down there, I would surely never manage to get up again.'

'That's hilarious. When you allow that side of yourself to shine, you really are fun to be with,' Olivia snorted.

'I'm not sure whether that's a backhanded compliment, but I'll take it as such.'

'So, Ma, if you're sure that you're definitely going, Ollie and I will be there to support you. I could even stay the night before and drive you.'

'When did I say that I was going?' Edna's voice was really brittle.

'I'm sorry, I must have misunderstood,' said Viola, backing down.

'Thank you, but if I decide to go, I am perfectly capable of ringing Mr Timms and asking him to drive and wait for me. I shall need to pay him to wait because I will have to go into the hall for tea after the service. After all, it would be very rude not to,' she added hastily.

'You don't want to go but say you must, and then you care about whether not staying for tea would be construed as rude. I give up.'

'Well, for a start, I will be parched and longing for a cup of tea, and they will probably have bourbons and custard creams.'

'Mother, they broke the mould after you were born!' Against their will, both girls broke into simultaneous fits of laughter.

Edna was not amused and sat scowling at them whilst they nursed their mugs of tea, trying desperately to make conversation, which in the end sounded so stilted and staged. They truly loved each other but were so different that it was hard to find common ground.

Eventually they left, leaving Edna so wound up about the impending funeral and whether she should go or not, let alone the unsatisfactory meeting with the girls and that unpleasant surprise visit from Edward Clitheroe. She decided to call for an appointment to ask the doctor for some more of those 'calming down pills' that he had given her after Don died. From time to time, he dispensed a top-up and she was running really low now. She could kill two birds with one stone by asking for a follow-up on the urine test that he had asked her to do.

She also decided that as soon as she returned, it was time to do a little detective work and find out why the wretched man wanted her house.

Edna dialled the number. 'Hello, Edna Watson here. I should like an appointment with Doctor this afternoon, if you would be so kind.'

'I'm afraid that he doesn't have a free slot until next Monday.'

Don't you get on your high horse with me, you sanctimonious cow. I pay my NI and taxes, and therefore I pay your salary, and therefore you will do what I want and not the reverse. Edna was outraged and responded, 'Next Monday! No, no, no, that will never do. I suggest that you look at the diary again.'

'As I say, we have nothing available until then.'

'Well, we shall have to see about that!' Edna slammed the receiver down and, not one to accept defeat, this woman on a mission grabbed her hat and coat and marched down to the village.

She entered the waiting room and frowned. The place was full of alarmingly unhealthy-looking people who were going to expel their nasty germs all over her. This called for desperate action.

'Next!' the receptionist with corkscrew curls and Coke-bottle glasses announced to the room.

Edna, with her arthritic legs, miraculously jumped up and hobbled across the room, pushing her way past a poor old lady with a walking frame.

'That will be me,' announced Edna authoritatively.

'Name? Date of birth? Address?'

'Edna Watson, Rose Cottage, Frimlington Green, Sussex, and old enough to be your grandmother.'

'Hmm, I don't seem to have you down. Is that Mrs?'

'I most certainly am still a Mrs, even though my husband choked to death on a chicken bone, or do you not have a space for that on your prefabricated form?'

Ignoring Edna's rudeness, the woman returned, 'What time did you say your appointment is supposed to be because I have no record of it?'

Edna thought the receptionist would have been better suited to working in the Unemployment Benefits Office, as she had heard how officious they could be.

'My appointment is *now*,' said Edna cheekily, using her favourite party trick of turning up for appointments that she didn't have and brazening it out. It had worked many times before, but today was not looking promising. Most unusually, Edna might just have met her match.

'But I don't see your name here,' the woman responded.

'I would say that is your problem, not mine,' said Edna determinedly, staring at her with her unnerving steely eyes.

The woman was now getting exasperated, and a group of unhappy campers had started to tut and twitch. 'Let's start with why you are here, Mrs Watson.'

Edna whispered to the counter, head down as if praying.

'I can't hear you, Mrs Watson.' The woman's patience was being tested to the limits.

Realising that she was getting nowhere, Edna decided to relent. She leaned forward and, in an ever so slightly louder voice, said, 'It's a "you know what" test.' She uttered the words so quietly that even she could hardly hear what she had said.

'I need to know what kind of test,' said the woman, with clearly better hearing than Edna.

'A quantum physics test,' shouted Edna sarcastically.

'What exactly seems to be the problem, Mrs Watson? I have all these people to attend to, so you need to tell me why you need to see the doctor, and I need to establish whether your need is urgent.'

'I am having a cardiac arrest and I need a triple bypass, so yes, I would say that it's urgent,' Edna barked at her.

'Rudeness will get you nowhere. Do you see that sign? Aggressive behaviour will not be tolerated.'

'I refuse to tell you in front of all these nosy so and so's,' said Edna belligerently.

'I'm sorry, but for the last time, you need to tell me what sort of test.'

'Well, you're a woman, aren't you? What don't women like discussing?' Edna was getting extremely agitated.

The woman, being particularly difficult and a most worthy opponent for Edna, appeared to be enjoying the sparring match. 'Mrs Watson, you must state your reasons right away or go and sit down.'

'Well,' Edna said with as much gusto as she could muster, 'the plumber said that there may be a problem with my waterworks, and he needs to test the system!'

'If you insist, I will squeeze you in at the end of the session,' the receptionist said, her lip quivering and trying desperately not to laugh, 'but Doctor will have to see these other people first.'

Edna had no choice but to take her seat amongst all the malodorous and wait. Finally, she arrived in front of the doctor, who smiled at her warmly.

'Now, Edna, what's going on? It seems like you gave my receptionist quite a hard time. Not very nice, that, is it?' Edna just sat there, giving him one of her most disquieting stares. 'Now, why don't you tell me what it's all about?'

Edna started to cry. Doctor Frome was the only person who ever saw this side of her.

'I am going through a very upsetting and stressful family issue, and I can't seem to shake the worry off. I don't want to tell the girls the details and they just keep badgering me.' At this admission, Edna started crying again. 'Most times I am burning up as if someone lit a fire in my feet and it's rampaging through my body. I can't sleep and I am just so tired.'

'Tell me about the crying, Edna. How often is this happening?'

Edna sniffed and went on, 'Most days. I just feel so sad and very, very angry.'

'So would you say that you have a temper, too?' the doctor asked kindly.

'Yes, I seem angry with everything and everybody. As you know, I have never been the most tolerant of people, but just lately… well, I scare even myself.'

'Tell me about the heat in your body,' he went on.

'I am on fire numerous times a day. It starts with a fizzing in my feet and ankles and works its way up. It even enters my head. Oh, and I wake up at night drenched in perspiration when I have my nightmares.'

'OK, Edna, I think you are going through the menopause again.'

'What?' she said incredulously.

'You remember that you had to stop the Hormone Replacement Therapy after the breast surgery? It's unfortunate, I know, but I think you need some help. First things first, I need to check that I am right. Roll up your sleeve and let me take some blood. I am going to write you up for a course of HRT, but I don't want you to start it until the results are in, when I will hopefully be able to confirm that it is definitely what you are suffering from. I also want you to discuss the implications of re-starting HRT with your daughters. The risk of re-occurrence of your kind of breast cancer is small, but it is there. You need to weigh up the quality of life that you are missing against the smallest infinitesimal risk of going through breast cancer again.'

Edna blew her nose loudly and finally stopped crying. 'So, do you think that this is what is wrong with me? Am I going to feel better?'

'Well, my dear, it's not going to turn you into a shrinking violet, but I do think you will feel a lot calmer and better equipped to deal with whatever it is that is upsetting you so. I'll call you when the results are through.'

If her knees would have allowed, she would have skipped out of the door. She wasn't even considering the risk; if she could start the therapy again, she was going to say yes.

She had become so lazy about cooking, and the amount of stodge that she was consuming was having a very adverse effect on her stomach, making her look at least six months pregnant. 'And what about my big stomach?'

'My dear, you need to cut out the carbs.'

Edna gave him an old-fashioned look. Well, she was absolutely and definitely not doing that! Totally oblivious to the advice, she stopped at the café and ordered a cheese and tomato toastie. Licking her lips and feeling a whole lot better after devouring it, she then ordered a slice of mille-feuille. *All this buttery pastry oozing with cream and jam is just what the doctor ordered, ha-ha!* Edna was definitely in one of her more naughty and feisty moods.

Back at the Trident offices, Edward Clitheroe was having to tell his boss that pest control had not been successful. He had mistakenly thought that the mouse would terrify the difficult and obstructive woman into submission, but he was proving no match for Edna!

'What do you mean, she wasn't scared? All women are scared of mice. What's the matter with you?'

'I'm telling you, Reg, she's got nerves of steel and quite unsteadies me, I can tell you. The game's up. She somehow figured out that I had something to do with it. Then she rapped me over the knuckles with her broom.'

'What are you, a man or a mouse?' Reg was getting very impatient now. 'I think you should go and join your furry friend. You remember, stupid? The mouse that was supposed to scare that blasted woman looks like it had absolutely no effect at all. You're pathetic. Now pull yourself together, prove that you're a man and get that terrible woman to move! If you don't, I'm going to have to reconsider your position and get someone with some guts. Go away and don't come back until you've sorted it.'

A distressed Edward sat down on a park bench. He was literally shaking and had absolutely no idea how he was going to convince that woman to move. Desperate, he called Benny again and implored him to make sure that this time she was really, really scared.

Edna returned home, kicked off her shoes, discarded her drab grey raincoat on the hall chair and sat down in the sitting room to watch *Countdown*. During her last shopping outing, she had found a new shop called Cook and spent a happy hour looking through all the freezer chests. Eventually she bought the lasagne, and it was this that she selected and placed in the oven after beating the contestants at their own game. Thirty minutes later, she was happily tucking into the creamy and scrumptious meal, complete with hot garlic bread. It was very easy to clear up, and she decided to sit down and watch the gorgeous Stanley Tucci. 'You're not jealous, are you, Don? It's only a bit of fun, and he wouldn't be interested in your Edna anyway!' Edna chuckled as she watched her heartthrob. She then decided to take a hot chocolate and two custard creams to bed and call it a night. She was so exhausted and slept so soundly that she didn't even hear the mouse greedily devouring her biscuit crumbs.

CHAPTER SIX

Sunday

EDNA WOKE WONDERING what to do with her day. In reality, she was very lonely and craved company, but bizarrely she squashed any attempt at kindness. It was as if she would push you away before you did it to her. The hours stretched ahead of her long and lonely since Don had gone, and she tried very hard to keep them occupied, particularly Sundays, which were by far the most difficult to fill. This in itself was strange because she had no friends, so whether people were busy doing their own thing at the weekends really should have made no difference, as all the days merged into each other. That is, except for her 'secret' outings, which always had the ability to make her feel better and at one with the world.

One of the things that she hated most about Sundays was that she normally had to forego her bath in favour of a shower because it was hair wash day.

Today Edna decided to leave her problems behind her and go mad and make herself a proper breakfast. Fried tomatoes, mushrooms and eggs with some hot buttered toast. Her mouth was watering. *To hell with the washing up!* She sat down ready to enjoy her feast, relishing every mouthful. Once finished, cradling her mug of tea, she then proceeded to read the *Mail on Sunday* and the *Sunday Times* from cover to cover. Having a most inquisitive mind, even if she had no interest in a subject, she still read every article. There was not a subject anyone could raise upon which Edna did not have an opinion, which made it all the sadder that there was hardly anyone to debate these days. Her son-in-law disliked her and, if she were totally honest, her daughters didn't seem crazy about spending time with her either.

She began the arduous chore of clearing it all away before she went upstairs, leant over the bath, and turned the faucet on. After running the water and checking the temperature, she stepped into the bath. Edna loved the experience of feeling squeaky clean. She poured a few drops of Youth Dew in and inhaled that familiar scent. She immersed herself in the creamy water, closed her eyes, and again travelled back in time. She was five years old and had woken so excited at the prospect of going to the zoo with her aunt and uncle. Although not appropriate for the outing, she insisted on wearing her favourite party dress, a white tuille concoction with a ballerina skirt embroidered with little pink rosebuds and, of course, her adored doll and surrogate sister Peggy had to come along too. Edna was going to be collected at two o'clock straight after lunch, but she was already dressed by eight o'clock that morning.

'Will I be able to see the giraffes?' she asked, tugging at her father's trouser leg, but he was heavily engrossed in the newspaper.

'Oh, I expect you shall, and perhaps the monkeys too. See if any of your relations are in there!' he laughed, teasing her.

Every five minutes, she asked if it was yet time to go. She kept looking longingly at the clock, willing the hands to move, and so it proved to be a long and boring morning. Finally, the doorbell chimed, and Edna ran excitedly to the door. This was going to be the bestest day of her life. She didn't care too much for for her insipid and boring cousin Felicity, but it was going to be such a brilliant day that it didn't matter if she came too. How sad that within an hour it turned into the most awful day of her life.

Edna opened her eyes with a start. She decided that, after her neighbourly visit, today would be a good day to see her father. She stepped out of the bath carefully, dried herself quickly, and selected a dress from the wardrobe. Once dressed, she made her way to the bus stop. It was only a short journey and Edna was full of trepidation at the thought of visiting her father after such a long time. She felt guilty at her prolonged absence, but she always justified it by being so horrified at the thought that her father, the man whom she had idolised, had been incarcerated for misappropriating clients' funds.

Edna walked into the nursing home, a far cry from the terrifying place where she had once visited her mother, as a frightened and confused twelve-year-old. There was no noxious smell of antiseptic and all the staff seemed cheerful and friendly. She entered her father's room, which was small but perfectly functional, with a picture of Elizabeth II hanging proudly over his bed. She surveyed the sad and pathetic man looking at her with a bewildered face. He was thin, with jowls where his neck used to be and very little hair, which was now salt and pepper grey. His pyjamas were clean and pressed, and generally he looked very well cared for.

Jittery and nervously fidgeting with his hands, still displaying his old habit of pulling at his fingers, he peered at her. 'Who are you? What do you want?'

'It's me, Daddy, Edna. How are you?'

'Do I know you?' Her father was getting more and more agitated.

'Yes, Daddy, I'm your daughter, Edna. I've come to visit.'

'I don't think I have met you before.'

She was heartbroken, remembering the handsome and funny man that she had adored. As she studied him, she decided that there was no point continuing to harbour this terrible anger that she had felt against him since he and Iris had divorced. Fighting back the tears, she remembered the cheese and tomato sauce sandwiches, the trips to Brighton with its pebbly beach covered in tar, devouring chips with salt and vinegar out of newspaper, being buried in the sand on the beach in Le Zoute, Belgium, and endless cuddles and laughter on his lap. Sometimes and possibly unkindly, their fun seemed to be at the exclusion of Iris, such was their intensely special father-daughter relationship.

'Do you work here?' Richard's voice jolted Edna back to the present.

She tried to stroke his hand, but Richard recoiled, and she swiftly thought better of it.

Hesitating only for a moment, she replied, 'Yes, I've come to tidy your room.'

Sad as it was, there was no point trying to explain who she was. He was too far gone and so she may as well take the opportunity to look through his things. Starting with the top drawer, to her embarrassment she found intimate items like pull-up pants and so, trying to preserve his dignity, she quickly closed the drawer again. Similarly, the other drawers and shelves revealed only personal items and nothing of interest. Then, remembering her own secret hiding place, she sent her eyes to the top of the wardrobe. She reached up, and after fumbling around at the back, her hands settled on a box. She opened it hungrily, heart thumping and there, under a pile of photographs, she found a bundle of envelopes bound with a rubber band and all with the same postmark: New York. She was shaking and desperate to go home and read them, but she felt guilty about not first spending some time chatting with him. Edna was so sad as she looked at this stranger- a stranger who had once been the most important person in her life.

She knew that she had been unkind by refusing to visit Richard whilst he was in prison and now in this nursing home, but she had been unable to forgive his behaviour to Iris. Now, looking at this pathetic creature, she felt guilty about her treatment of him. After all, he had been an amazing father and maybe if she had been kinder, he would not have succumbed to dementia. Who knew? Whatever, she decided that as difficult as it might be, she had to start visiting her father regularly.

Lost in thought, she had become unaware that Richard was rocking backwards and forwards, moaning and wringing his hands. Startled, she realised that he had started yelling at her and demanding that she get out of his room. A nurse entered and tried to soothe him, but he was getting more and more distraught. The nurse mouthed to Edna that it was probably better that she left, and Edna was shocked to realise how relieved she was to be able to end the visit. The memory of the day she had visited Iris in the psychiatric hospital all those years ago was flooding back with a vengeance and it was just too painful.

She stuffed the envelopes into her bag and almost ran to the bus stop.

Fiercely independent, Edna was still heaving her trolley onto the bus for her weekly shop. Today she needed some eggs and milk, and so as much as she wanted to get home to read the letters, she decided to pop into Aldi first.

Yet again completely ignoring the advice the doctor had given about eating healthily, she bought a beef and mushroom pie from the deli counter to warm in the oven for supper. Having found everything on her list, she wheeled her trolley, whilst managing to negotiate her walking stick through the car park, which was a quick cut-through to the bus stop. Almost at once a scruffy young man tapped her on the shoulder, waving a ten-pound note.

'You dropped this,' he exclaimed excitedly at her in broken English. Edna knew that she hadn't dropped it and, as sharp and astute as ever, she denied this firmly.

'It's not mine and you know it. Now be off with you before I call the police.' The man was trying to push the note into her bag, insisting that it was hers (which she knew was a very old scam), whilst really trying to get at her wallet. Quick as a flash, Edna took her trusted walking stick and, for the second time that week, rapped a man over the knuckles. The man ran off screaming in pain, dropping the note in his haste. He could be heard shouting, 'You've got my ten pounds!'

Edna stood in the car park and, realising that as compensation for her trouble she could now pay for a taxi home, let out a very loud belly laugh.

Back home, after yet another most unhealthy lunch, this time a toasted tuna and cheese sandwich, she washed her plate, but only rinsed her mug so that she could have her second cuppa in the sitting room. Then she peeled off the rubber band and started to read. Slowly the terrible truth emerged, and she was shocked to realise that to the contrary, Bill had not deserted Iris. He had written many pleading letters to her, even offering to move to London if she would only speak to him. Edna skimmed over the endless protestations of love and references to their lovemaking, feeling like a voyeur, but the last letter that Bill had written completely devastated Edna, and she doubted that she would ever be able to erase it from her mind.

✍

My dearest Iris,

It breaks my heart to realise that you really have made your life without me, but I hope that you have found the happiness you deserve. I can't blame you, because our relationship was doomed, and none of it your fault. You had to put Edna first and I well understand that, but nevertheless, I cannot live one more day without you.

I have made arrangements for Helen's continued care for as long as she lives. Andrew is an adult now with his own family and financially, I have left him well provided for. And so, this is the last letter that I shall write to you.

I have never loved anyone the way that I love you and I want you to know that the short time we spent together was the happiest of my life.

I hope that everyone can forgive me for what I am about to do but without you, my darling, there is just no point.

With all my love, always and forever,

Bill

᪐

The tears were pouring down Edna's face. If only her mother had known the truth. As she read Bill's letter over and over again, the reality that it was too late to turn the clock back made Edna overwhelmingly sad and racked with guilt. She had unwittingly played a major part in her mother's unhappiness and ultimate death. The realisation that Iris had died heartbroken and dejected, never really knowing how much Bill loved and adored her, was too much for Edna to bear. It was quite obvious to her that her mother would never have married her second husband, Alfred, an awful man that Edna had loathed, if she had not felt so alone. That if the father whom she had idolised had not been so cruel and selfish, things might have been so different. As if the whole wretched affair were not bad enough, Edna found one last letter written in a different but somewhat familiar hand. It was a diatribe written by a distraught son who blamed Iris for his father's suicide. He told her that Bill had been unable to live without her, the love of his life, and that by cruelly ignoring his pleading letters containing protestations of Bill's undying love, she was, according to this young man, totally responsible for his father's death. He told Iris that Bill eventually took matters into his own hands and, after settling his affairs and making sure that his wife would be well cared for to the end of her days, he had walked to the Hudson River just before midnight, filled his pockets with stones and rocks, and jumped off into the icy cold and unforgiving waters. There were a few passers-by, but it was all over before they could do anything. The police were called, and divers finally retrieved his cold and ravaged body. Bill's son went on to remark what a cruel and heartless woman Iris was and how he would never forgive her. But thanks to Richard's devious ways, like the love letters that had preceded it and the tragic farewell note Bill had posted before he took his life, the letters had never been read until now, too late for Iris. The irony was that Bill had left his wife anyway. Edna was crying uncontrollably at the injustice of it all.

She was thinking about what a scary time it had been for Iris, but now she realised what a frightening and confusing time it must have been for Bill. No one knew of his existence and so no one had notified him about Iris's internment in the nursing home. Edna decided that she needed some escape from all the information that was rolling around in her brain.

Them the phone rang.

'4742.'

'You'd better get yourself some extra security, missus. Coz you're gonna need it.' Edna went quite cold. Dealing with a mouse was one thing, but this kind of aggression was more than even she was equipped to deal with. Still, she managed to muster her courage and barked back at him:

'And if I were you, I would get some security for yourself!' All said with a confidence that, in truth, she did not feel. Yet there came a sharp intake of breath; the shock she sensed on the other end of the phone was almost palpable. 'Oh, and thanks for the advice, but you can tell your boss that I have my own minder and he's watching *you*! It's going to take a lot more than you're doing to scare Edna Watson!'

The line went dead.

After watching but not concentrating on the rest of the afternoon TV and news, she couldn't believe that it was already six thirty, and so went into the kitchen to warm her beef pie. After demolishing it, she cleared away and sat down to watch TV again. She was still feeling so horribly unsettled and full of guilt at her behaviour towards her mother, but she was also distressed to think that Bill had died a most horrific and undignified death because of her father's actions.

After only an hour of TV, the details of which she couldn't even remember, Edna dozed off and eventually woke an hour later, feeling again as if someone had lit a fire in the soles of her feet that went on to rage through her body. She walked into the kitchen, opened her fridge and stood there, pushing her scorched body as far into the open door as was possible until the fire was extinguished, and only then made her way upstairs for another lonely night. Clutching her mother's book, she was torn between needing to know what happened next and not wanting to read past the point of no return. Finally, exhausted after yet another day of disturbing revelations, she closed her eyes, and within ten minutes, she was fast asleep.

Chapter Seven

Monday

MONDAYS WERE VERY busy and satisfying days. Edna opened her eyes and swung her legs over the bed. *Mustn't be late. They'll be waiting for me.* Then she remembered that she had an appointment with the dentist, the prospect of which always evoked horrible memories of when she was a small child. The mere mention of the word brought back visions of rubber masks and worse. She went downstairs to the kitchen to make herself a scrambled egg, something she rarely made because it involved washing a frying pan; Edna being very lazy when it came to anything culinary. She merely glanced at the paper, as she was not in the mood for reading about the world's problems. Her own troubles were far more pressing, and she was absolutely exhausted after yet another disturbed night flinging off her bedclothes. At one point she had entered the bathroom and doused a flannel in cold water, which she then applied to her head, the insides of her wrists and the back of her neck. Overtired and miserable, she then crawled back into bed to try to catch another few hours' sleep.

After breakfast, she made her way into the bathroom; but today was not going to be a relaxing bath ritual. She was still feeling anxious about her visit to the dentist and as soon as she lay back in the bath and closed her eyes, she was a helpless child again. She could see the dentist in his stiff white coat and the nurse in her blue uniform, both trying to drag her out of the lavatory. She fought as hard as an eight-year-old could, but inevitably, and not for the first time, they managed to force her into the chair and place a foul-smelling rubber mask on her face. If a psychiatrist had been asked to observe Edna, they would have concluded that her repetitive thoughts and dreams were mainly about being out of control and being forced to do things against her will.

Since she was a small child, she had always feared hospitals. Not surprising, really. When she was three, she needed to have her tonsils removed. Her parents took her to an ugly building with a hideous smell of antiseptic, where a very stern lady with a navy dress and white starched hat sent her off to the playroom, 'while I talk to your parents'.

That was the last Edna saw of them until post-operation, when she was due to go home. She pined every day of her enforced confinement, refusing to eat on the pretence of a sore throat, and she resolved to pay them back for their cruelty when they did eventually return. If they returned. How could she know what had actually happened? Of course, Edna later discovered that her parents were devastated not to be able to say goodbye, but this ghastly woman, in her misplaced wisdom, forbade parents to have any contact until discharge, lest they unsettle the children. No doubt the unfriendly woman wanted to avoid creating work for herself, being better qualified as an overzealous Sergeant Major than an empathetic care giver. Remembering their promise that they would say goodbye, Edna blamed her parents for leaving her in the horrible place without even a kiss, and so once home she didn't speak for days, wanting to punish them. Another theme that a psychiatrist would have observed was Edna's desire to punish people who hurt her.

The mere smell of the rubber mask as she lay on the operating table, fighting not to go to sleep, was still so vivid in her memory. The legacy of this was that she had always hated visiting people in hospital, deigning only to visit close family or friends when not to do so would seem uncaring or callous. In these difficult circumstances she always looked straight ahead in case she was to see something that would scare her. Even now she found the machines so formidable and the rooms always freezing cold.

At the age of four, Edna fell and cut her head open. She was bleeding and crying for her mother, who was spinning around in a panic like an over-excited puppy. After calling the doctor, her anxious mother ran outside screaming for help and as soon as the first person arrived, she left her small, frightened daughter in the care of a neighbour and ran outside again.

'Where is my mummy? I want my mummy. Why doesn't she stay with me?' Edna remembered asking.

The confused neighbour, a young woman who lived next door, just cradled her, whispering gently to soothe her as they waited for the doctor to arrive. Their family doctor, a tall, slim, elderly gentleman with kind eyes and a gentle manner, wanted to send Edna to hospital, but given her wretched experience with her tonsillectomy, she flatly refused, kicking out, with her hands and legs wildly thrashing. Reluctantly the doctor put some steel clips into Edna's scalp and gave instructions to Iris as to what to do if the wound started to bleed again. He reminded her to make an appointment to have them removed in seven days and walked out of the door shaking his head in utter disbelief at Iris's inability to cope with the drama.

As Edna grew up, she realised these were the first indications that her mother could not cope with stress and worry, and she saw the adverse effect this had on her development. Edna wanted to be able to rely on her mother. She wanted her mother to be the safe place that she could turn to when things went wrong, but the reality was that Edna had to be the grown-up, and over time, she grew to see that Iris was such an anxious little thing, more like a child than a parent, and she had to be the one looking out for her mother. Love her as she did, Edna resented it like hell. However, she had to admit that she herself had not always been a good mother, and maybe this was the reason why.

Edna actively disliked her name, especially after learning that the only reason she was so named was because her maternal grandmother, Edith, and her mother, Iris, had been fans of Edna Deane, an actress who became famous for being the inspiration for the song 'I've danced with a man, who's danced with a girl, who's danced with the Prince of Wales'. It was too stupid to be saddled with such a name just because of that, she complained bitterly.

A lonely but much-loved only child, Edna was never without her doll, Peggy, the surrogate sister that she so ached for. Edna hated being 'the only one', but Iris told her that her maternal grandmother had lost three babies before Iris was born, and so once Edna came, Edith had convinced Iris to be grateful for what she had and not to try for any more children. Iris had told Edna that, as a dutiful daughter, she had done as her mother commanded.

What Edna couldn't know was the unimaginable shocking truth about what really happened. The truth that lay hidden in her mother's journal.

And so it was, that in lieu of a sibling, Edna had taken her relationship with her adored doll, Peggy, to the extreme, insisting that she was her sister and that a smaller version of everything she ate be placed in front of the doll, only to be hungrily devoured by Edna when no one was looking. Peggy was her confidante, being the only one privy to 'the incident' that was always lurking in the background. As soon as she was old enough to understand, Edna vowed that if she were fortunate enough to be able to have children, she would not stop at one child. As events turned out, however, for Edna it was quite the wrong decision.

Edna's normally unruly hair was limp and flat, but today there was no time to do anything about it. *It's a flipping nuisance, but I'll do it when I get home. I mean, it's not as if I fancy my dentist or want to impress him, for goodness' sake!* She chuckled at the thought of it. Sadly, the thought of fancying anyone at her age was cause for great amusement. Without even realising it, she had missed out on a great number of good years.

Steeling herself for the dreaded visit she made her way into the hall, donned her hat and coat, and walked to the dentist. If she had been going anywhere else, she would have been happily munching on a Kit Kat or similar chocolate treat along the way, but even Edna's greedy nature knew better than to do so before having her teeth examined. She walked through the village, head down, noticing nothing and no one, and finally, a very sullen Edna walked into the dentist's surgery.

'You're not your perky self today, if I may say so, Mrs Watson.' The dentist could tell that she was out of sorts. 'Are you feeling OK? Is there anything that I can help with?'

'No, you may not say so, and there is absolutely nothing that I wish to discuss with you other than the state of my teeth,' she snapped at him. 'Now, if you don't mind, I would appreciate your getting on with it, as I am extremely busy today.'

The dentist, well used to Edna's terse behaviour, asked her to take a seat and he lowered the chair.

'Open wide, please.' Luckily for him, now with her mouth so wide that he could almost see what she ate for breakfast, she was unable to say anything, so he continued his examination, checking all her molars. 'Any pain? Anything unusual? Exactly how much sugar do you consume in a day?'

She got the feeling that he enjoyed the opportunity to throw questions at her, knowing full well that she couldn't answer with so much paraphernalia in her mouth. Finally, after she thought that the pain of holding her mouth wide open for so long would never leave her jaw again, he gleefully announced at the end of her torture, 'All good, Mrs Watson. We'll see you again in six months.'

On the way home she popped into No 7, letting herself in with her entrusted key. 'Hello, my love. How are you doing today? I got you some nice tomato soup and a crusty roll. I'll just pop upstairs and make your bed and then we can have a nice little chat.' Edna was starving and, in truth, couldn't wait to make her way home, but she knew how much her little visits meant and so ignored the growling within. She made a mental note that maybe, in future, she should buy enough for two, so that they could sit and enjoy lunch together and she wouldn't be so desperate to get home.

As Edna busied herself tidying the sparse bedroom, she couldn't help noticing the family photo given pride of place on the well-worn chest of drawers. Two smiling and proud faces, with their arms around a smug young man complete with cap and mortar board and a surly-looking blonde girl to complete the picture. Who were they? Edna mused. Most likely his children, but you never could tell. Whatever, the fact remained that they were absent, and why? The poor man had to rely on the kindness of strangers and that just wasn't right. She knew that she shouldn't judge, but she couldn't help thinking that such a sweet old man could hardly have done anything so awful as to warrant this apparent desertion. Then she wondered if maybe she was being too hasty to condemn. Had they died in some awful earthquake in Peru or on a capsized boat on the Amazon, devoured by crocodiles? Edna just loved to make up stories about people. It made her normally boring life so much more interesting.

Finally, after sitting with him and recounting the story about the horrid Edward Clitheroe, she made her way home. Unable to wait to prepare anything, she greedily demolished a bag of Tyrell's lightly salted crisps, a banana and a chunky Kit Kat and moved into the sitting room. With a long afternoon stretching ahead of her and not much else to do, she wanted to read more of her mother's journal, but she couldn't concentrate, and her thoughts again wandered back to the past.

✥

As a child and later an adolescent, Edna always observed rather than joined in and never initiated conversation. Although her parents told her that she was really pretty, she was never popular with the opposite sex. It seemed that the boys preferred personality to good looks, so she spent her time going to art classes, wandering around museums, collecting miniature perfume bottles at department stores with her best friend Daisy, voraciously reading books, going to the cinema, and dreaming about meeting 'the one'.

One day Daisy arrived at Edna's front door, her eyes red raw and watery.

'Whatever's the matter, Daze?' Edna was really concerned because Daisy was always laughing and smiling, never crying. This must be something really awful.

'We're emigrating to Australia!' Daisy blubbed. 'They told me last night and I haven't slept a wink. I said I won't go, and they just insisted that I would absolutely love it and soon make new friends. I don't want new friends. I want you, Edna,' and at that statement, Daisy collapsed into another wave of convulsive sobs.

Edna was traumatised. She was blinking profusely and trying to take it all in. How was she going to live without Daisy? Australia! Well, she may as well be dead for all the difference it would make. At this thought, Edna started crying uncontrollably and they both held onto each other, frightened to let go.

Only three months later, Edna was standing at Heathrow waving goodbye to Daisy and, although they promised that they would meet up in the school holidays, they both knew that this would never happen. It was totally impractical. Australia was just too far! They both knew that it was over and at that moment Edna hated Daisy's parents almost as much as she hated Uncle Harold and Aunt Betty.

Edna spent the next four years focusing on her schoolwork as she had nothing else to distract her. She just ambled through, dreaming and still hoping to meet her dream man. Then finally, when she was twenty, her life truly began. At this Edna smiled as she remembered how she had met Don.

It was her Aunt Betty and Uncle Harold's twenty-fifth anniversary party, and she had flatly refused to go.

'You have to go,' Iris pleaded. 'Your aunt and uncle will be so upset if you don't!' Of course, her mother could never have imagined that those words were like manna to Edna's ears. As she had kept her feelings hidden from her parents, they had absolutely no idea that she still bore such resentment towards Betty and Harold. As far as her parents were concerned, and probably the offending couple themselves, the incident was long since forgotten; but for Edna it could never be, and the thought of making them upset in any way just reinforced her desire to stay home. Thankfully for Edna, Richard, normally quite a placid man, insisted that she meet him for lunch, whereupon he sternly told her that it was her duty to go.

'What do you mean, you won't go to your aunt and uncle's party? Why do you dislike them so?' It seemed that Richard and Iris had definitely managed to erase the fateful day completely from their minds. Edna supposed that for them, the reality was just too awful to contemplate.

'I just don't want to go,' she said sulkily and looked away.

'Listen to me, young lady, you are going, and I won't take no for an answer. I know you're disappointed in me, but he's my brother and I am still your father,' said her father, most uncharacteristically. Edna knew that he meant business. She knew that out of respect she had no choice but to acquiesce, and so it was that she met Don, opening up her world beyond her wildest dreams.

She woke on the morning of the party and contemplated faking flu but wasn't sure that she could pull it off and so grudgingly began to get ready. She had beautiful silky brown shoulder-length hair that thankfully just needed a careful brush. She laid her makeup out on her dressing table and remembered how Daisy had helped her get ready for her thirteenth birthday party all those years ago. The memory still made her sad. Firstly, because that was when she first saw her father's feet of clay, but also because Daisy was now a fully-fledged Australian and Edna still missed her best friend terribly. Turning to the job in hand, she selected a black-and-white geometric tunic top with black flares from the wardrobe, held it against her and stared at the reflection in the mirror. She had to admit that she did look rather good, but quickly acknowledged that there really wasn't much point. Who was she dressing for anyway?

The party was in full swing when she got there and she stood feeling surly and grumpy, surrounded by what felt like hundreds of alien people, all of whom seemed to know each other, wondering why on earth she had given in to her father's command. Everyone was apparently involved in animated conversations, and she desperately wished that the ground would open up or someone would shout *Fire! Evacuate the building!* so that she could escape the misery of being what felt like the last girl standing. Then Felicity came over, dragging a most gorgeous young man in tow.

Edna, meet Don, my old friend from university.'

Edna had to stop her mouth from dropping open, *most ungainly,* when she caught sight of him. He was of medium height, and to her, he looked like a cross between Steve McQueen and George

Peppard. He seemed to encapsulate both actors, but of course it was all just in her head. He was wearing a silver-grey plaid suit, a blue paisley tie and Chelsea boots complete with Cuban heel, and Edna simply couldn't take her eyes off him.

Edna had never understood what Don could possibly have had in common with such an ineffectual wimp as Felicity, but thankfully he did. He asked Edna to dance, and at that moment she was supremely grateful to Richard for having taught her the rudiments of dancing at that party all those years ago. She was hesitant to start, but Don took the lead and by the end of the evening she had felt that she was Ginger to his Fred. They never stopped talking and were delighted to discover that within their interests they had so much in common. Books, cinema, theatre, galleries were all things that they both enjoyed doing.

'Have you ever seen *The Mousetrap?*' he ventured.

'No, but I have been wanting…' Her voice trailed off. What should she say? If she said that she wanted to go, did that constitute begging for a date? If she showed no interest, would he take that as a secret sign for *No I don't want to go out with you*? She had no experience of this dating game and felt trapped in a hole with no way out.

'Would you like to go? I could get tickets,' he went on.

Edna's hands felt clammy and damp and she could hardly get the words out fast enough. Her, a date. Her, with this deliciously handsome man. At last, she found her voice again.

'Yes, thank you. I would love to.'

'Good stuff. I shall call you tomorrow and let you know the details. I have some studying for exams that I need to pass, so should we say next Saturday? And if there are no tickets, we could meet for supper anyway, and arrange another date for the theatre.' Don stopped suddenly. Edna was anxious but needn't have been, as it was just his turn to be insecure. She didn't know until he told her later that he also was struggling with being too forward, talking about a second date before they had embarked on the first.

Don asked to take Edna home, but she explained that she was with her parents, all the while secretly wishing that she didn't have to go home with them and potentially miss what could have been her first kiss. She tossed and turned that night, unable to sleep with excitement, and practising that longed-for and seriously overdue kiss on her pillow. She had seen enough films, and by the end of the week, her pillow practice had been quite productive. She just needed the opportunity to put it into actual practice. Lying there, unable to sleep for excitement, she thought that it was so surreal, like some pathetic girly novel.

Over time Edna discovered that she and Don were so perfectly matched, even though they were so different. Where Edna was strong and resilient, Don was gentle and easy mannered. Over the next six months they fell completely head over heels in love with each other, and as the relationship bloomed, so did Edna. In those early days, she truly felt that without him she couldn't breathe and with him she could conquer everything.

They went ten-pin bowling, where Edna always beat Don. At the cinema, she cried her way through *Doctor Zhivago* and laughed out loud at *Airplane*, especially the bit where the air hostess managed to unhook the patient's oxygen with her guitar. They spent hours listening to Carole King and James Taylor, and Edna was fascinated by Hockney's exhibit at the Tate. They wondered at the Parthenon sculptures at the British Museum and enjoyed long walks in Hyde Park and Richmond Common. Their kisses became more passionate and urgent, but they always stopped short of actually consummating their relationship. As they both lived at home, it was not too hard to stick to their principles.

Nine months later, sitting at La Poule au Pot in Pimlico, Edna was staring at Don and wondering why he looked so decidedly uncomfortable.

'Pass the butter, would you?'

She studied him more carefully and thought that he looked decidedly liverish despite the fact that he appeared to be ravenous. She watched Don butter the bread thickly, looking like a twelve-year-old child who would be more at home happily tucked up in bed with the latest issue of the Beano. It seemed, for Don, that adulthood was not proving all that it was cracked up to be. At least, tonight it wasn't.

'You're very hyper tonight, Don. Everything OK?'

She could see that his eyes were fixed on his plate, and she was so worried that he was going to break up with her. It was only years later that he admitted what was really going on in his head. She smiled as she remembered the conversation.

'I was trying desperately to calm myself, wrestling with my innermost thoughts,' Don told her. 'I could feel the perspiration running down my back and thinking that the level of anxiety I was feeling was surely enough to bring on cardiac arrest. I looked around anxiously to see if there was any information about a defibrillator, which is all so visible in America. I have always had mild hypochondria and been totally enamoured with my television hero, Dr Kildare. When I visited my cousins in Long Island, I was so struck by the idea of defibrillators. Did you know, Edna, that by law even the lowliest establishment had to have such a machine? Well, there was no such luck at *La Poule au Pot*, and I panicked, not knowing where the nearest hospital was. I tried to focus on how beautiful you looked and to remember my speech, but I had been diverted from the impending conversation which was getting terrifyingly closer. All I could think was: How long could a person last after the onset of an attack? Could they get me to hospital in time? I was willing myself to the present and to stop the nonsense, but I couldn't. Having always been taught how to behave, I could hear my mother's voice ringing in my ears, telling me that if I were to undertake anything in life, I was to make sure that I gave it my best shot. Well, I was desperately but unsuccessfully trying to do that!'

Don went on to tell her that at that point he had been struggling to contain the bile that was fervently trying its hardest to embarrass him, and that he had wished he had not eaten so much of the rich garlic butter, which was rapidly formulating an image of rancid liquid in his head. What had he been thinking? He had felt completely trapped, and doubt had taken over. At that point he had not been sure that he shouldn't abort the plan and try again when he was feeling braver.

'But then you told me that I had said I had something I wanted to talk about and that you were all ears. I knew then I had to go through with it.'

At this point, Edna remembered that Don had taken a deep breath. Inside, she had been screaming, *Oh no, don't break up with me.* Nothing could have been further from the truth because, as Don later explained, actually what he was doing was willing his stomach not to let him down but to behave.

She giggled fondly as she remembered the 'big proposal'.

'Err, the thing is…' His voice had trailed off. He cleared his throat and started again. 'The thing is that we have so much in common. We enjoy the same food, music, restaurants. We are self-sufficient and I truly have strong feelings for you. I was just wondering whether you might… mmmm… consider… ermmm…' A small cough and then he blurted it out, 'Whether we should think about getting married.'

It had all come out wrong. He told her afterwards that his prepared speech was actually, *Edna, I have loved you since the first time I saw you, standing there looking so lost. I have spoken to your father and asked his permission… Will you marry me?* But unfortunately for Don it had all come out miserably wrong.

It didn't matter that Don had bungled it. Edna dropped her fork, tears running down her cheeks. No matter that it was not the most romantic of proposals. It was a proposal and one that she had been praying for.

'Oh Don, you can't imagine how long I have waited to hear those words. I'm so glad that we saved ourselves for this moment. Yes, yes, of course I'll marry you, you silly duck.' She was crying with pure joy.

It appeared that Don was so overcome with relief that she had said yes that he suddenly suffered an extraordinary pain, clutched his chest, and yelled, 'I need a doctor,' before collapsing over the table.

All they remembered was the sight of boeuf bourguignon spilt across the table, waiters running around in a panic, and the ambulance team complete with crash cart trying to manoeuvre their way through the tiny restaurant, knocking over chairs, wine, and anything else around, to get to the 'dying' patient. Once the crew had heard that he was in the midst of a proposal, it was all that they could do not to crack up laughing in front of him.

Once they had been reassured by the paramedics that it was, in fact, a panic attack, a clearly embarrassed Don called for a taxi to take Edna home.

The next day, Edna and Don cracked open a bottle of champagne and celebrated with their respective parents, all of them delighted. Richard and Iris were evidently happy that Edna had chosen such a wonderful boy from such a fine and upstanding family, which was all that they could ever have hoped for their daughter. Don's parents seemed totally enamoured with Edna. On the other hand, it was apparent they were not so crazy at the prospect of being connected with Iris and Richard, particularly Richard. There was not much love lost between the two sets of parents, but it didn't matter, because they all had the end goal in focus, which was to see their children happy.

Over the years Edna and Don laughed like drains at the thought of the two of them in the most romantic restaurant in London during one of the most exciting moments any young couple will ever have, whilst Don thought that he was having a heart attack.

Edna went into the kitchen. She made herself a cup of her favourite 'builder's tea', selected two biscuits from the rapidly depleting biscuit tin, settled down again in the sitting room, and picked up her mother's book.

᠊ᠪ᠊

June 1975

It was hard planning the wedding that should have been so joyous for me and now just served to remind me how useless my own marriage had been. That is, except for Edna.

I drew on my small savings (much to the relief of Richard's empty pocket) and after a small and intimate ceremony for only immediate family and friends at the very beautiful Grosvenor Chapel, the wedding party moved to The White Elephant on the river in Grosvenor Road. The room looked absolutely lovely, adorned with white hydrangeas, roses and peonies. Richard welcomed everyone and made a carefully worded speech, thanking me for raising Edna so beautifully and showering her with such devotion. At this I was fighting the tears and nodded at him, grateful that he did publicly acknowledge my efforts to keep it all together.

My little girl, you looked so beautiful, and I am so happy with your choice of husband. I know that Don will always look after you and you both seem the perfect love match. Hopefully a much better match than Richard and me.

My eyes filled with tears of happiness as I remembered the day that you came into my life, which was undoubtedly the best day of my life.

⤜

Reading this, Edna was a little uneasy at her mother's strange choice of words, describing the day that she had 'come into her mother's life'. It seemed odd, and rang a distant bell, but hastily dismissing it she turned aside from her mother's journal for a moment, looking back fondly on her own memories of her wedding. Richard had thanked Don for being the best thing that had ever happened to Edna and had politely thanked his parents for their support and love towards their new daughter-in-law. He then proceeded to talk about his adored daughter Edna. And there it was again....

'My dearest Edna, the day that we got you was the happiest day of my life. Looking at the beautiful young woman you have become, I think that Mummy would agree with me that we definitely got something right.

'Through all life's ups and downs, you have been my constant, my raison d'etre, and I am so proud to be your father. I don't think that I am going to say any more, because I am feeling so emotional, but all I ask, my darling girl, is be happy. You have chosen a wonderful husband, and I couldn't have wanted a finer son-in-law. Thank you all for coming and making this such a wonderful day.' With tears streaming down his face, Richard sat down.

Edna had pushed the strange and vexing niggle to the back of her mind and continued to enjoy her special day.

The wedding breakfast consisted of smoked salmon with brown bread and butter, roast rack of lamb followed by the restaurant's famous chestnut mousse. Richard had carefully chosen the wines to suit Iris's pocket and had saved the champagne for the speeches. Don's brother, Roger, made a really wonderful speech to the happy couple. Then Don stood and made his speech.

'Mother, Father, thank you for always being there for me and for taking Edna to your hearts. We know that the closeness will continue forever. Iris and Richard, thank you for giving me your precious daughter. I promise that I will always love, cherish, and take care of her. Thank you also for the splendid lunch today. And now I come to the love of my life, my darling Edna. You have made me the happiest man alive, and I promise that I will dedicate the rest of my life to making you happy. You look absolutely beautiful and radiant, and I am just the luckiest of guys.'

This was the cue for the little trio to open with 'The best is yet to come'. Don led Edna to the dance floor, and she nestled into his chest, not quite believing what had happened today. She was now Mrs Edna Watson, married to the most wonderful man on earth, and she just couldn't wait for the next chapter of what she knew would be their amazing life together.

After making their farewells, Edna and Don spent their wedding night at The Savoy, courtesy of Don's parents. Edna had never stayed in such an opulent hotel, yet it was all so very tasteful.

The manager showed the excited couple to their suite and Edna could not believe her eyes. They entered the lobby, and the manager opened the double doors to the sitting room with a flourish. There before them was the most magnificent view of the Thames; they were both completely overawed. The room was beautifully furnished with blue damask draped curtains, gold velvet squishy sofas, and even a piano, complete with a vase of long-stemmed red roses and a bottle of Dom Perignon champagne. At this point, they couldn't wait to get rid of the man so that they could explore the most important room of any honeymoon. They were absolutely ravenous, having not been able to eat the lunch for excitement, and called room service, ordering a light supper of tomato soup and dover sole with mashed potato, after which they fell asleep exhausted and were most disappointed to wake at 1.00 am to find they had wasted a good deal of their wedding night sleeping. Again, they rang room service and ordered the famous peach melba, originally created for Dame

Nellie Melba, and finally began their honeymoon proper. Edna woke the following morning, looked round the room, and blinked a few times to convince herself that it had all really happened. Don asked if she would like room service for breakfast, but Edna shook her head.

'No thanks, I may never stay in a hotel like this again, so let's go downstairs and enjoy the full experience.'

Edna walked into the dining room, her first official outing as Mrs Edna Watson, totally bursting with pride. They both ordered the full English to see them through the journey and, two pots of coffee later, the luggage was loaded into the taxi which took them to Heathrow airport. They waited in the terminal to board their BEA Trident flight to Marco Polo Airport Venice, and Edna was so excited that she felt she could fly the aeroplane herself.

Edna had enjoyed family holidays to Belgium, Le Touquet, and even Italy, but never anything like this. She had never experienced such luxury, such excitement at all these new experiences.

On arrival they were collected by a water taxi and whisked off to the Cipriani hotel close to St Mark's square where they enjoyed five days of pure bliss.

They woke each morning taking the hotel launch to St Mark's Square, venturing out in search of the most welcoming bars, gorging on delicious steaming hot cappuccinos made with that sweet Italian milk, and dunking the Italian version of mini baguettes, then sucking off the wet foam, leaving a tell-tale moustache. Don arranged everything to make his 'princess' happy. They went exploring St Mark's Square. He organised a Riva speedboat so that Edna could sample the wonders of Venice as they should be seen. He hired a gondolier to serenade them along the canal. They watched glass ornaments being made in Murano and examined the exquisite lace of Burano. Whilst there, Don took her to a wonderful little restaurant that had been recommended to him called the Gatto Nero. They ordered a simple but perfectly executed risotto which they thoroughly enjoyed, washed down with an ice-cold glass of Soave. Sitting outside on the canal side terrace, surrounded by lovely geranium plants in front of the beautiful quaint little buildings, each one painted a different pastel colour, Edna was overcome with joy, knowing that she could never be happier than she was at this moment. Each night they feasted on different and exquisite delicacies (previously untasted in England) such as fried artichokes, veal Marsala or ossobuco, always finishing the delicious meal with something like juicy peaches sliced with squeezed lemon, or sweet oranges with a moist almond cake. They drank Sambuca, excitedly watching the flame disappear and peach Bellinis, which made Edna deliciously mellow and giggly. At lunchtime they wrapped their mouths around panini sandwiches, or tried the famous vitello tonnato, at an authentic trattoria. They would then find a prettily painted cart selling soft creamy gelato, a different flavour every day.

'You're going to make me fat!' she squealed with delight.

Back home in England, they settled into a loving routine. Each morning, ready for work at the stockbroking firm in the City, Don kissed her goodbye, looking so dapper in his three-piece suit, and every time she heard his rich brown velvet voice utter, 'Until tonight, princess,' she would melt like ice cream that had been left in the sun for too long.

Then the girls arrived, with their inevitable crying and dirty nappies, and Edna's mood changed. She loved her children but just couldn't enjoy the simple pleasures of motherhood. She was nervous every time the girls did anything that didn't involve sitting quietly on the floor with a book. She could well imagine the neighbours laughing behind her back at the sight of Viola, aged four, plodding like a spaceman, one foot in front of the other, announcing, 'Careful!' after each step.

With the stress of motherhood, Edna's moods intensified and

not for the better. Eventually, she and Don settled into a comfortable pattern but sadly, for both of them, with no more passion. Because of her hatred of being an only child, she had vowed that if she were so blessed, she would not have fewer than two children, but truth to tell, not being a natural mother, she might have fared better if she had stuck at one. Who knew in those days about post-natal depression?

As the girls grew up, Edna noticed that they tended to turn to each other instead of to her. She wondered if it was because she gave them no understanding of why she was so difficult, at times distant and, some would say, even remote. Accepting of the way it was, they just went about forming their lives without the normal motherly presence that most girls would take for granted. Olivia, being the eldest, was headstrong and quite bossy, whilst Viola was easy-going and initially happy to follow her elder sister's lead. However, once they passed puberty, they were so different that they followed their own aspirations and became more removed from each other's lives. Olivia was spoiled and self-centred, going through men like discarded fruit slightly past its sell-by date, whereas Viola was, in truth, a much nicer person, and the nicest of the three women. They were all damaged in some way though, without ever realising that their characters had been formed indirectly by Edna's traumatic childhood experience. Maybe if Edna had tried to seek help in the early days, things might have been different; but she didn't, and that was that.

⁓

Edna saw another mouse scampering towards the kitchen. Quick as a flash, out came the broom and the Marigolds, after which the mouse suffered the same fate as his friend. 'I have to do something about that wretched man. Why is he trying to scare me?' she asked the silent house. 'What is it about my house? There's more to this than he's telling me. But what?' Wearily she sat down at the computer. The puzzle of Edward Clitheroe was weighing so heavily on her mind that she had to find out what he was up to and why he wanted her house. She started by typing Rose Cottage, Frimlington Green, Sussex into Google. It didn't take her long to find out what was going on as the predictive text took over.

SUSSEX BOROUGH OF FRIMLINGTON GREEN

PLANNING AND SUSTAINABLE REGENERATION DEVELOPMENT MANAGEMENT

SUSSEX COUNCIL ARE INVITING COMMENTS ON THE APPLICATIONS LISTED BELOW WHICH ARE ADVERTISED FOR THE REASONS GIVEN:

21/04205/FUL DEMOLITION OF EXISTING HOUSE AND ERECTION OF 2 TWO-STOREY SEMI-DETACHED HOUSES WITH ACCOMMODATION WITHIN THE ROOF SPACE AND A ROW OF 3 TWO-STOREY TERRACE HOUSES WITH PRIVATE GARDENS, ALTERATIONS TO THE EXISTING VEHICULAR ACCESS, PROVISION OF 5 PARKING SPACES AND ASSOCIATED CYCLE AND REFUSE FACILITIES.

Edna was dumbfounded. They were applying for planning permission for her house! *How dare they? They are going to rue the day that they ever messed with me.*

She dialled the local police station.

'Wilmington Green Police station, how can I direct your call?'

'I should like to report a possible fraud.'

'What's your name?'

'Edna Watson,' she almost barked.

'Err, is that Mrs?'

'Why does everyone want to know my marital status? What difference does it make to a crime?' Edna was getting overexcited and irritable.

'OK, Mrs Watson, let's try and calm down, shall we?'

Edna gave a deafening blow of her nose. 'Don't you patronise me, young man. I can tell by your voice that you are just a whippersnapper.' Edna was in full flow now and there was no stopping her.

'Now, now, Mrs Watson, I'm going to have to ask you to calm down and remember that you are talking to an officer of the law.'

Edna backed down and, most uncharacteristically for her, she actually apologised. 'Forgive me, but I am so distressed.'

'One moment, and I will put you through.'

'Wilmington Green station, Officer Croft speaking.'

Edna was relieved to be talking to someone in authority and began to recount her sorry story.

'Edna Watson here, from Rose Cottage. I want to report a crime. I am being bullied and worse.' Normally calm and controlled, Edna was fighting to get the words out.

'OK, Mrs Watson. Let's take it a little slower, shall we?'

'I received a phone call from a man… I say man because I could never call him a gentleman… and he said he wanted to see me about my house. I still don't know why I agreed to see him because I have no intentions of moving, and actually told him that when he came the following day. He was dressed, as my father would have said, like a 'spiv', and I detested him upon sight.' Again, another loud blow, and then she continued. 'I threw him out, leaving him as to no doubt about my wishes. Then two days later a mouse appeared in my bedroom. I stunned it and threw it out onto the drive. The following morning the man appeared again with no appointment, whereupon he began to detail all the reasons why I should sell. In his eagerness to convince me, he talked about unwanted visitors and even mentioned some friend of his. I then realised that it must have been he who planted the mouse in my house. And now, today, I have just encountered another one!' Another exceedingly loud blow before she went on, 'Anyhow, I decided to go on the Internet to see what I could find out as to why he wanted my house, and there it was. An application for building consent. Only I didn't apply for it.' At this, she started crying profusely again. 'Now a horrid man has made a threatening phone call to me. I tell you, it takes a lot to unnerve me. I have been through a lot in my life, but this is just too much.'

'Well, I'm really sorry to hear that, and I think we should send some officers round to take a statement. I would say come into the station, but given that it does concern your house, it might be more prudent for us to visit you. It's a bit late for today, especially as we have the Save Wilmington Green Post Office march today. Would first thing Wednesday morning be OK?'

'Thank you so much. I don't mind admitting that I'm really scared and, as people who know me will testify, it takes a lot to rattle me!'

'Well, if anything changes or you get any more incidents, call us, and we'll drop everything and make you a priority.'

Next, she looked up the number of Roberts & Roberts family solicitors. She moved to the hall, lifted the receiver, and dialled the number.

'Roberts & Roberts, how may I help you?'

'Good afternoon, my name is Edna Watson, and I should like an appointment urgently to thwart a potential fraud.'

Edna could almost hear the sharp intake of breath as she imagined the telephone receptionist sitting up and paying attention. She imagined the poor girl had not encountered any excitement since 2001 when the vicar was found at the back of the public toilets, looking like a bad impersonation of Dame Edna Everage in a dress he had sneaked out of his mother's wardrobe. It was all over the local gazette at the time, and quite a scandal for Wilmington Green.

'How about three o'clock tomorrow afternoon?' Edna could tell by the speed at which she was given an appointment that the woman couldn't wait for a bit of juicy gossip. Edna was also sure that the local gazette probably paid well for tip-offs.

Edna replaced the receiver and made herself a cup of tea and a cheese sandwich. Not in the mood for anything else, she made her way upstairs for another troubled and restless night.

CHAPTER EIGHT

Tuesday

EDNA OPENED HER eyes and just lay there feeling very anxious again.

'What is happening to me? Threatening phone calls, men trying to cheat me out of my home, rodents in the bedroom!' All said sadly to the absent Don. She felt as if she were in a B movie that she would never watch. She then went into her bathroom, stared at her reflection in the mirror and, with monumental effort, the feisty Edna returned.

'They are not going to get away with this,' she yelled at the mirror. 'They picked the wrong person this time, and I will make sure they pay.' With that outburst, she went downstairs, walked into her kitchen, and decided on bran flakes for breakfast.

'Nice and easy this morning, Don. I don't have time to waste. I will tell you what it's all about once I know what I am doing.' She was so preoccupied with plotting her revenge that she almost poured the milk onto the newspaper, instead of onto the Weetabix. No matter, as she didn't intend to read it, having far more pressing things on her mind. Maybe she could lead those villains up the proverbial garden path. The irony of that made her giggle. Yes, of course, she would pretend that she was interested and get them involved in lots of fees and time wasting, only to change her mind once the police were able to take over. *Mm, I need to check with Mr Roberts whether that would prejudice my case.* Despite her agitation, Edna had still not lost her razor-sharp reasoning.

Her mind was working overtime and eventually, thoroughly exhausted, she gave up and went upstairs to draw her bath, but today, try as she might, she just couldn't relax. As she soaped her right breast, she looked down at the scars and was taken back to the moment that every woman dreads…

Then she lay back, closed her eyes and allowed herself to be transported to another time.

Whilst drying herself all those years ago, Edna had felt a little lump in her right breast the size of a pea. Trying not to panic, as she had had some false alarms previously, she visited her GP the following morning. He was gentle and fairly reassuring.

'It doesn't feel like a cancerous growth, but let's book a mammogram just to be sure.'

He went on to explain that a palpable lump should always be investigated, and how right that was. The following day she was sitting in a hospital waiting room, studying all the other people and wondering which of them was going to be the latest statistic. *Just so long as it isn't me.* She closed her eyes and silently prayed to her maker, which was a most uncharacteristic thing for Edna to do.

She tried desperately not to look at all the people coming and going. Some were unbelievably walking around with drips attached to a trolley and yet still smoking. She stared intently at this dismal scene and remembered what her mother had once remarked in a different scenario: *This is not a community I want to be part of.* Now she totally understood how her mother had felt that night at Gamblers Anonymous.

The woman opposite was crying, and Edna studied her face, trying to read what was going on behind those terrified eyes. Edna was so intrigued by this person that it took her mind off the icy fear that gripped her so tightly. She didn't know whether the woman was crying for herself or for a loved one. It was impossible to tell. She looked healthy *but you never know...* Edna deliberated whether to ask her if she was OK – or would that be intrusive? After five minutes, she took the plunge and went over to the woman.

'Excuse me, but I was just wondering if you would like some company?' This was Edna at her very best, showing her compassion in all its glory. 'If you would rather not, I won't be offended. You don't even have to speak; you could just gesture for me to leave with your hand.' The woman looked up at Edna with wonder.

'Yes, that's very kind, thank you.' She went on to tell Edna that she was waiting for news of her father, but because of the pandemic, they were not allowing her to be with him. He had suffered a stroke and was unable to communicate. He was just flailing his arms with a look of panic in his eyes. 'You see, I promised him that whenever his time came, I would be with him at the end, but they won't let me in, and I know he'll be terrified. Due to the Covid lockdown, at ninety-six, he was washing his own kitchen floor because he wouldn't let anyone in, including me,' the poor distressed woman went on. 'It appears that he slipped backwards onto his head.'

Edna took the woman's hand and gripped it tightly. As difficult as Edna could be, she absolutely shone with compassion and kindness when the occasion called for it.

'Listen, you may not get this chance again. Just go and make a complete nuisance of yourself. Cry, rage, and scream until you get what you want. This is absolutely inhumane, and you must not let them get away with it. Otherwise, you may regret this forever.'

The woman got up and, with renewed energy, made her way over to the receptionist, but as she wandered off, Edna's name came up on the electronic noticeboard, which she felt was far more suited to an airport, indicating that she should report to the second floor. She felt bad about abandoning the woman, but there was really nothing more that she could do.

Edna made her way upstairs and again took her seat in yet another anonymous waiting room.

'Edna Watson,' the radiographer called out and smiled kindly at her.

Edna stood up, feeling decidedly queasy, and allowed herself to be ushered into a room. 'Hello, Edna, I will be taking your pictures today. Please could you take everything off from the waist up.' Edna took a deep gulp and, realising that there was no way out of it, gingerly removed her top and bra.

She stood there feeling vulnerable and, yes, ridiculous in her trousers and boots, yet naked from the waist up. Knowing that she couldn't do anything to cover her modesty, she swallowed hard, doing her best not to think about what was happening. One of the few wise things that the counsellor had imparted to Edna all those years ago was, 'If you find yourself in a situation that you find abhorrent, just become a potato, go with the flow and feel nothing.'

Edna had never been comfortable with others seeing her body except for Don (and even then, it had taken time), so she steeled herself, took a deep breath, walked to the large and unforgiving machine and followed instructions.

The kind young woman placed Edna's right breast onto the metal plate, asked her to stand still, and then, after a lot of shuffling around, finally brought the top plate down, squeezing her poor bosom to within an inch of its life – or that's what it felt like. She likened it to a cheese sandwich when it was placed into the toasting machine and the top plate was clamped shut. It was soon over, and she was asked to go and wait outside. After about half an hour, anxiously studying all the other women and pondering their fate, she was asked to enter another room. 'Look, Edna, we have seen something, which may be nothing, but we would like you to have an ultrasound just to be sure.' Edna began to feel that her luck was running out as she lay there on the hard couch, trying desperately not to be anxious. For all her misery caused by missing Don so much, she realised that even with the possibility of meeting up with him again, she was not yet ready to leave this life. The first part of the procedure was not unpleasant. Just more embarrassment, lying there with her bits on show and horrid sticky and cold gel smeared over them. If ever she had missed Don and wished that he were with her, it was now. *Pull yourself together, Edna, Don isn't here, and you have to be strong.* The radiologist asked Edna if there was any history of breast cancer in the family. 'Absolutely nothing,' Edna said with great confidence, thinking that must be a good sign. Unfortunately, that feeling didn't last long, as he told her that he could see the lump and honestly did not know what it was, so he wanted to do something called a core biopsy, which to Edna sounded horrific.

'When will you do this?' Edna tried not to panic.

'We'd like to do it now, Edna. If that's all right with you? I will inject your breast with anaesthetic, and I promise that will be the worst part. After that you'll feel nothing. Just a lot of pushing and shoving, and each time we take a biopsy, there will be a loud clicking noise; I promise no pain, but you do need to lie extremely still.'

Edna tried to relax, desperately hoping that the end result would be worth it, but a sense of foreboding came over her. By this point, she was past being embarrassed by the process of yet another man other than Don seeing her in an undressed and undignified state. She only wanted to be OK.

The nurse was stroking her head and asking if she was OK and telling her how well she was doing. On the face of it such minor things, but Edna was, not for the first time in her life, feeling scared and vulnerable, and at the age of seventy-four she finally acknowledged that every little kiss and stroke did make a difference. *Yes*, she thought, *there really is incalculable value in the kindness of strangers.*

Edna looked into the nurse's eyes, which had obviously seen so much, and had smiled so warmly at goodness knows how many women in need. She told Edna that her name was Halina. *Was she born with this empathy?* Edna wondered. Finally, the procedure was over, and Edna was asked to pop her clothes back on and wait outside to see the doctor, a professor, no less. After what seemed like eons, but was probably only ten minutes, the professor calmly and gently explained that he agreed with the radiologist that they did not know what it was. It could be benign but, in any event, whatever it was, it should come out! Edna was all for that. After all, she reasoned, no one wants a squatter in their body. She told them that she was happy for them to evict it without delay. The professor explained that they would need to wait for the result of the biopsy to come in order to diagnose whether it was, in fact, breast cancer and told her that they would be in touch as soon as they received it.

The wait was interminable, especially as Edna would not tell the girls unless she had to, but finally, two days later, they asked her to come in. Of course, she knew the moment that she entered the room, even before the surgeon had uttered a word. One didn't need to be a nuclear scientist to know that it didn't take two surgeons and a specialist nurse wearing a badge that clearly announced what she was doing there to say that everything was clear, and so Edna sat there quietly, whilst being told that this was indeed early stage 1 breast cancer but grade 3, which meant that it was very fast growing but still perfectly treatable. At that moment, her life stopped. Although everyone must worry and feel anxious beforehand, Edna didn't believe that anyone really thinks that they will hear those terrifying words.

'You have cancer.'

Totally unprepared, she certainly didn't expect to hear the diagnosis and all she knew was that 'it' was not going to win and that she was going to eradicate 'it' from her life.

The specialist breast nurse then took her into another room and explained what the next few months were likely to look like. They wanted her to go the following day for a full body scan (PET) to make sure that it had not spread to other parts of her body. She explained that they laced the dye with sugar because cancer cells attach themselves to sugar, and Edna felt sick. Always having been a sugar addict loving biscuits, cakes, chocolate, tomato sauce and desserts, she was not going to find it easy going cold turkey on the sugar, if indeed she ever could. The next stage would be a special enhanced MRI, followed by other necessary pre-op procedures.

Now it was real, and Edna had to tell her two daughters that she had breast cancer, albeit with every hope of a full recovery. The truth was that she desperately wanted their support, but could not bear the thought of worrying them, and she certainly did not want pity. After all, she was a survivor, not a victim. She made her way home, a complete mixture of shock and defiance.

As Olivia was the eldest, Edna dialled her number first. Her heart was thumping as her daughter answered.

'Hello, dear, I was wondering if you could pop over and see me.'

'What's up, Ma? You sound strange.'

'Nothing dreadful, just something that I want to go over with you and Vee.'

'If it's about money, we've told you time and time again, we don't want you fretting. You spend it and if there's anything left, OK, but we don't want you to deny yourself and end up the richest person in the graveyard.'

Edna was exasperated. 'No, it's not about money, and instead of trying to anticipate what I want, can't you just say yes?'

'Of course. I didn't mean to upset you. I could pop over in the morning, or if you need to discuss this before then I could come over tonight. Is Vee coming?'

'As my eldest daughter, I have rung you first, and my next port of call is Viola.'

'OK. I'm flexible. Just let me know when she wants to come. Ma, I'm just thinking, would you like me to come over now anyway?'

'No, no, thank you. One of us will let you know what Viola says. Bye, dear.'

'Hello, Viola, it's Mummy.' This was Edna's gentle persona. 'There's something that I want to go over with you and Olivia. When would you be free to pop over?'

Edna could hear the sharp intake of breath, followed by, 'How about seven o'clock this evening?'

'That would be perfect. Would you be a love and tell Olivia?'

'So you've already spoken to her?'

Oh my. This sibling rivalry is just exhausting. It's probably the best and only thing about being an only child. 'Only because she's the eldest, now don't go getting touchy with me.'

'No, of course not, Ma. See you later.'

Edna could tell that she had made both her daughters anxious, but there was no avoiding it, and she was doing the best she could under the circumstances.

Unusually, Edna had no appetite and just had some bread and butter and a cup of tea for lunch. She was unable to read anything or watch the TV, thinking about how she was going to reveal her news. She made herself another cup of tea, helping herself to a couple of digestives and at seven on the dot the girls arrived together, each looking decidedly anxious. Edna hurried them into the sitting room and, stumbling and hesitatingly, she opened the conversation.

'I went to the doctor last week because I found a lump in my breast.'

She watched her daughters exchange nervous looks.

'Anyway, I had the results of my tests today and the thing is, it seems that I have cancer.' The air was cold and sharp as Edna went on, 'I'm going to be absolutely fine, but I thought you deserved to know.'

'Deserved to know!' Olivia exclaimed. 'Mother, what are you talking about? Of course we deserve to know. We're your daughters and we love you.'

'How bad is it, really? Viola interjected.

'Well, it's stage 1, which is good as it means that it hasn't spread, but it's grade 3, which means it is very fast growing and so they want to operate immediately. I'm going to have it done in a few days' time. There are just some things they need to do beforehand.'

The girls were of course shocked, always believing their mother to be invincible, but they were hugely supportive too, trying to do what they could to help a mother who frankly didn't find it easy to be helped. It was just against her nature, her need always to be in control.

'We'll do everything to support you, won't we, Ollie?'

'Absolutely. We'll take you wherever you need to be. We'll stay with you when you come out. We'll look after you until you're fully recovered.'

'Hang on there. Please don't get carried away with yourselves. I am not and do not intend to be an invalid.' Then Edna realised how ungrateful she was sounding and hurriedly and graciously continued, 'But thank you, that's lovely of you; however, I won't need much, and I *am* going to be absolutely fine.' And then she giggled. 'After all, the world cannot possibly go on without me in it.' And they all laughed. A laugh which hung somewhere between hysteria and relief.

Ever practical, Viola mustered up the courage and asked, 'But actually, Ma, what are the odds of recovery? Do you know what the treatment involves?'

'They're going to do something called a lumpectomy, and hopefully it will be as little intrusive to my breast as possible. However,

I have told him he can do what he likes just as long as I am going to get over this. The professor is very confident that it's been caught in time and that I will be fine. In terms of after the operation, they won't know about chemotherapy and radiotherapy until they get the results of the biopsy.' She went on to tell them that the next day she was scheduled to have the full body scan and went on to explain what that meant. She tried to reassure them that the professor had said that, looking at the pathology report, he was not expecting any further problems, but needed to be sure.

The girls seemed to calm down after this and although terribly concerned, they were wise enough to know that they had thrown enough questions at their mother for one day. After Edna had reassured the girls that she was fine, but she really did want to be alone, they grudgingly left.

Even after the devastation of being told that she had cancer, Edna was concerned that she would be hungry. Having been told that she was not allowed to eat after six in the morning, she set the alarm for five and made herself some scrambled eggs and toast.

The girls arrived to accompany her to the hospital but were not allowed to sit with her due to the radioactive dye that had to be introduced to her body. The worst part was lying still for one hour on her own waiting for the dye to travel round her body, followed by another lonely thirty minutes on another hard table during the scan. She had just been given a terrible shock diagnosis and the last thing she wanted was to be alone with her troubled thoughts. Edna just tried to keep pushing her mind back to images of loved ones and how she was going to fight this and get better. Her efforts were rewarded. Two days later, she received the news that she had prayed -yes, prayed - for.

'Other than the little lump that we already know about, the scan is clear. We now need to press ahead with the preparations for the procedure.'

Completely exhausted, with nerves strained and taut, she allowed the girls to take her home and, after a cup of tea and an egg sandwich, help her into bed.

'Are you really sure you don't want us to sleep here tonight?'

'No, Viola, thank you, but I really do want to be alone.'

Reluctantly, the girls left, locking the front door behind them.

When she awoke the next morning Edna could still feel her emotions in play. It was the day before surgery was scheduled and oh, what joy! A free day! No one wanted to prod her, push her, stick pins in her, fill her with radioactive junk or stare at her exposed body.

Since the diagnosis, Edna had had an irresistible urge to clear out her drawers and cupboards filled with articles on a multitude of subjects, receipts nearly as old as her, a dog-eared copy of *How to Write a Book*, photographs, menus, and general junk that her family would just chuck out without a thought if she were not there. She quickly pushed that inconceivable thought from her mind. The process was, she thought, a bit like nesting when she was pregnant. She had this urge to get everything in order so no one would talk about her in a shocking way, heaven forbid the doctors should be wrong about the prognosis. Edna was actually very positive and even arrogant because she really could not believe that the world could possibly go on without her, but nevertheless… Just in case…

She was going out for lunch with the girls, and she was secretly delighted that they had arranged it. She had called Mr Timms to take her, but before they could even set off, Edna had a row with *the ignorant and illiterate oiks* who had blocked the road with a load of junk furniture, completely stopping them from getting out of the road. They, of course, were on the receiving end of all the anger that had been building up inside Edna since her diagnosis. Once on her way, she asked Mr Timms why he had chosen this particular *long-winded* (these words uttered silently) route. He told her that it was not his fault that Edna had argued with the removal men, to which she had a good mind to say, 'I've got cancer – what's your excuse for being cranky?' But she let it go. She and Mr Timms had been comrades for many years and in their dialogue behaved like an old married couple, which could not be further from the truth. Although he was paid to drive her, they were indeed old friends.

Finally, she arrived, and the girls were there waiting for her.

'Hi, Mother, how lovely to see you, but you do look a little pale.' The instant that the words came out, Olivia frowned with obvious regret. Edna noticed Viola shoot her sister a warning glance.

'I'm perfectly fine.' Edna retaliated with a bravado that, in truth, she did not feel. 'I just didn't sleep well last night.'

'Of course you didn't; that was really thoughtless of me. Sorry, Ma.' Most times the girls called Edna Mother, but occasionally, when trying to be more affectionate, they called her Ma. However, whenever Olivia and Viola were talking about Edna, they usually referred to her as Ma.

The *Casa Maria* restaurant was in the next village to Frimlington and the girls had chosen the lovely Italian trattoria, knowing that Edna liked it. The room was comfortable, the staff friendly but unobtrusive, and with none of the pomposity of *La Maison*, which of course was one of Olivia's favourites. Edna sat in between Viola and Olivia and tried to relax. *They are really trying to help, so come on, Edna, buck up and try to enjoy it.* She looked at the menu and decided to go for minestrone soup, followed by veal Milanese with sauté potatoes and French beans. As anxious as she was, her appetite was still enormous. *Well, I won't be able to eat tomorrow, so best get some reserves in.*

'James has got into Oxford, Ma, and I am just so proud of him,' Olivia said. She had managed to secure the school fees as part of her divorce settlement. 'Joe is paying, of course. I mean, it's no skin off his nose, as he is James's father, after all, and anyway, it was the least he could do after going back to Marilyn like that.'

'That's brilliant, Ollie. I wish I could say the same about Lucy. She has absolutely no interest in academia. After all that we invested in private schooling, I think she'll end up going off to be a beach bum!' Viola said gloomily, stirring her soup endlessly yet not touching a drop. 'One thing's for sure, I can tell you we're not funding it!'

Edna was not actually enjoying the day because she felt so wretched, and she was relieved when lunch was over. She felt guilty that they had gone to such effort, but she just wanted to be in her own familiar surroundings. Olivia dropped her home, but Edna didn't invite her in.

'I just want to be alone and quiet,' Edna said weakly. 'I hope that you understand.'

'Of course, Mother, I'll be here at six in the morning tomorrow to collect you. Just think, it will soon be over, and you'll get your life back. Sleep well.'

Thinking about the day, Edna allowed herself to acknowledge (only to herself, of course) just how tired she had been lately, and she actually couldn't wait to get up to the bedroom and rest. For months now, she had been waking up exhausted, as if she had not slept, but had always put it down to stress and her raging fires. Now she knew there was another culprit adding to her discomfort, she vowed that its days were numbered.

Edna woke on the day of the surgery with the adrenalin going at a pace. She was really ready for it. *Let me at it. I just want it banished and exiled from my life because it has NO place in mine.* Viola collected her on the dot of six o'clock, knowing that lack of punctuality would agitate her mother. Throughout the journey, Edna was fighting the turbulence within her, wanting to calm the unease she felt. They arrived at the hospital and a nurse asked Edna to dress in the obligatory hospital gown and elasticated anti-thrombosis stockings. The assistant surgeon then came and handed Edna two pages of 'things' that the attractive young woman explained could potentially happen. However, she was quick to reassure her that they were unlikely, and that Edna did need to have the operation as soon as possible. Viola wanted to know why they had to go into such scary detail, but Edna figured that it was more about covering their backs than anything that was likely to happen. Then the anaesthetist appeared and after checking Edna's blood pressure and other vitals, he asked her to sign the consent form and pronounced her 'good to go.'

'Edna,' said the surgeon, 'I am going to try to save your nipple, but the tumour is so close to it that I can't promise.'

'As long as you promise me that I am going to be at my grand-children's weddings, you can do what you like to me,' Edna told him with false bravado.

They wheeled her down to the anteroom. 'Just a sharp prick, Edna. Now you're just going to feel something cold going through your arm.'

Edna started to tell him that it hadn't worked, but the next thing she knew she was lying in her room again.

'Hi, Ma. It's all over, you're fine.'

Edna tried to focus but everything was a little blurry and she felt more than slightly woozy, but she did remember the professor saying, 'Good news, Edna, it's all out and I managed to save your nipple.' At this, Edna wanted to giggle. Of all the things that had worried her, her nipple was of the least interest.

Like everything else in her life, Edna took the surgery in her stride and was discharged the next day with a ream of instructions. She was being referred to Professor Ellis, who would be her oncologist, and a consultant radiologist, who would plan the course of treatment.

'So, Edna, please call me Paul,' were the first words that this lovely, cuddly teddy bear of a man uttered. He told Edna that she was extremely lucky that her cancer had been caught early because it had been very fast growing. She was so very grateful to hear that after a barrage of blood tests, for her kind of cancer, HER-2 negative, it would not be necessary to have chemotherapy, and even more happy when she realised that she would not lose her hair. How shallow, she thought, that in facing the threat of death, she could be so worried about such a trivial thing.

The whole family laughed when one of her grandchildren said, 'That wasn't so bad, Grannie, you only had cancer for three weeks!' Oh, the innocence of the young. It still brought a smile to her face.

A week later, Viola came to visit with her newly-born niece. They put a pillow on Edna's knees, laying the baby carefully on her lap, and she cried when she saw her. Edna was later heard to say, 'There is something miraculous about having cancer, with its inevitable fear of death, set against the beauty and innocence of a newborn baby, with all its life ahead. It's quite overwhelming.'

Six weeks later, after a delay waiting for the wound to heal, Edna embarked on a round of radiography like a trouper. First, she had to go for a 'fitting'. Feeling very anxious, she lay on the table whilst the two technicians meticulously prepared the coordinates with a red infra-red beam above her head. Then they marked, like a tiny tattoo, the exact place between her breasts so that the treatment would be directed with absolute precision in exactly the same place each time. The following week, she lay there perfectly still, as directed, whilst the technicians checked and re-checked meticulously until, finally satisfied, they moved to a glass booth whilst they started her surprisingly short and painless treatment. It felt like being in a scene from a science fiction film, with all the red beams shooting across her body in the dark, cold, and scary room.

The exhaustion she felt, which was cumulative over the weeks, was like nothing she had ever experienced, but she only needed to remind herself that there were people who were not thrown a lifeline, who were told that their cancer had spread too far, to stop feeling sorry for herself. She reflected on how blessed she was to be here, to think about the day before and plan the day ahead. So, five days a week, she presented herself at the hospital for her three weeks of treatment, and then she would be done. Before she knew it, those fifteen days of radiation, which seemed unremarkable (yet she knew were anything but), were over. Together with her scars, that minuscule tattoo was a permanent reminder of just how lucky she had been.

As fate would have it, Edna had actually lived through more terrifying experiences than most would expect in a lifetime. She used to think that if she were ever to write a book, no one would believe it. However, despite the way that she sometimes behaved towards them, the fear of losing her daughters was definitely the worst that life could possibly throw at her.

She dried herself carefully, selected a beige polo neck sweater and a pair of trousers, and made her way downstairs, as she could hardly wait to get back to her mother's journal. Deciding that she would just read a little more before her appointment with Mr Roberts, Edna made herself comfy on the sofa, or as comfy as one could be if you ignored all the lumps and bumps.

At two-thirty Edna made her way into the village and at three o'clock on the dot she walked into Roberts & Roberts and announced herself to the strange-looking receptionist.

'Good afternoon, Mrs Watson to see Mr Roberts,' said Edna in her most authoritative voice, sizing up the woman in front of her, who looked like she had been caught in a time warp as she was wearing a bottle-green crimplene dress, her hair dressed in Jean Harlow-style waves and fuchsia pink nail polish adorning her nails.

'Good afternoon, Mrs Watson. I will just let Mr Roberts know that you are here.'

Edna looked around the antiquated office. It was a family business, and she doubted that it had been decorated since the founder, old man Roberts, had passed away. *Well, it matters not in the least what state the building is in, just so long as he can help me with this.*

She looked up as she realised that the receptionist was talking to her.

'Mr Roberts will see you now, Mrs Watson.'

Edna could feel the woman's curiosity and even suspected that she was the type that would place a water glass against a wall to eavesdrop on a conversation.

'Ah, Mrs Watson. Do come in.' The man looked as if he had just stepped out of a Dickens novel, with his black suit, white wing collar shirt and a pair of pince-nez sitting precariously at the end of his nose.

'Please take a seat. May I offer you a cup of tea?'

'Thank you, that would be very kind,' said Edna, desperately hoping that tea meant biscuits too.

He banged his hand enthusiastically upon the bell on his desk and the poor receptionist, who was far too close on the other side of the door, nearly jumped out of her skin.

'Now, why don't you tell me all about it?' His voice was soothing and kind.

Edna began to recount the story, as she had told it to the police, and pulled out her hankie, giving her nose a very loud blow.

In an attempt to mop up her tears, Edna took a tissue from the box that Mr Roberts proffered, and then looked expectantly at Mr Roberts. She was frustrated that the crying was getting to be a habit these days.

After considering her tale of woe, the very proper gentleman spoke soothingly.

'Well! A most unfortunate story, I must say.' Mr Roberts was wringing his hands. 'But the thing is, my good lady, as of yet, you have suffered no loss in financial terms, although I hasten to add, in terms of peace of mind, you have suffered considerably.' Edna nodded in agreement. 'What I now need to consider is how we stop, and indeed if we want to stop, this application going through.'

At this, Edna looked extremely puzzled.

'I don't want to elaborate until I have had a chance to consider what should be your next move. I believe this is a clear case of harassment, and we need to restrain them. Whether that is a case for the civil court or the police to prosecute, at this stage I really cannot say. Even then, sadly, there is not always a guarantee of success. I just need a little time to consider everything. Look, I have started adopting a new idea which is called "no win, no fee". It means that if I can see more than a sixty per cent chance of winning a case, I act for nothing and take my fees out of the amount awarded by the court. How would you feel about that?'

Edna could hardly believe what he was saying. She hurriedly agreed in case he should change his mind. 'Yes, thank you, that seems eminently fair.' However, sharp as ever, she continued, 'And what exactly would be your fee if we win?' Edna wanted him to understand that she was no pushover.

'My fee would be based upon five per cent of what you received. How does that sound?'

'That sounds very fair. Let's get on with it.' Edna began to blow her nose again.

'Very well, Mrs Watson, I do believe we have a plan.'

'Please call me Edna.'

'As you wish, er, Edna.' She could see that he did not look very comfortable with this intimate form of address.

Much to Edna's glee, the tea and biscuits arrived and, after chomping her way through most of the plate and grudgingly realising that it would only be polite to leave him at least one sole sorry-looking biscuit, she thanked him and left to get on with the job in hand.

'Thank you so much, Mr Roberts, I look forward to hearing from you.' And out she marched with a far more confident stride than when she had entered the building. After stopping off at the local 'chippie', Edna hurried home with her cod and chips, which were smothered in salt and vinegar, accompanied by a large pickled onion and two slices of bread. Smacking her lips, she again tried to talk to Don. 'Ooh, that was just delicious, wasn't it? Let's go and watch *Who Wants to be a Millionaire?* and see what those half-wits come up with.—After answering nearly all the questions correctly, she switched off the TV. 'I'm just going to turn the heating off, it's like a furnace in here.'—She announced to the cold and empty room and then went upstairs. Within half an hour she was fast asleep – only to be woken three hours later by a raging fire within her bones. This was too strong for a wet flannel, and so one cold shower later, she dried herself and, totally exhausted, fell back into bed.

Chapter Nine

Wednesday

Edna was excited and just a little nervous about her meeting with the CID and decided to have a very quick bath. After a brief wash, she grudgingly stepped out of the tub, dried herself carefully, and selected a blue cowl-neck sweater and a pair of navy trousers. She had just finished getting dressed when the phone rang, bringing her back to the present, and with a leaden heart, she answered.

'4742.' Edna spoke into the phone hesitatingly.

'Hello there, Edna, it's David Roberts from Roberts & Roberts. Is this a convenient time to chat?'

'Of course, please go ahead.'

'Well, the thing is, having spent time looking through the file, I've concluded that even though you've been through hell, my good lady, the court are not likely to award you damages as you have not, most fortunately may I add, suffered financial loss. Distress and suffering is a very hard case to prove. However, the fact that they have applied for planning could well be in your interest. There is no way they can do anything without you, and you may just benefit if the planning were to be approved. You might want to think about this and the possibility of capitalising on the added value it would provide at a later date. The bully-boy tactics are quite another thing, and I am calling to inform you that this is definitely a case for the criminal court, and you should allow the police to move forward with their investigations.'

Edna swallowed hard. It was quite a lot to take in. 'Thank you, David. I really appreciate everything you have done for me, and please feel free to bill me for your time.'

'That will not be necessary but thank you for the offer. I was pleased to be of service.'

After thanking him profusely, Edna replaced the receiver, her mind whirring.

The doorbell rang and, after checking who was at the front door, Edna let the officers in.

'Please follow me.' Edna led the two men into the sitting room. 'Well, sit down then. I can't stand with my dodgy hip, and I can hardly sit if you don't.'

'Thank you, Mrs Watson, that's very kind of you.' The eldest of the two sat down. 'Now, in your own words, why don't you tell me all about it?'

'In my own words!' she exclaimed. 'In who else's words would they be?'

'Apologies, Mrs Watson. It's just a figure of speech. We would just like you to tell us what happened.' The second officer sat down.

'I've already done that!' Now Edna was getting irritable. 'I told Officer Croft when I called to report it. I assume that he wrote everything down. Can't he read his handwriting? This is absolutely infuriating.'

'Please, Mrs Watson. We realise this is a most distressing time for you, but to be sure that nothing gets left out, this is our way of ensuring no detail is missed. It just helps us to build a stronger case.'

Edna's shoulders dropped and she calmed down.

'OK then.' She repeated verbatim what she had reported at the station and during the discussion with Mr Roberts.

Upon hearing the details of the offer on the house, the mouse, and the threatening phone calls, the officers appeared to be taking Edna's complaint very seriously indeed. They made a call to the station and a special officer arrived soon after to make some modifications to her phone. He took a great deal of time to explain to Edna how everything worked and what she had to do.

'So, Mrs Watson, firstly let me say how sorry I am that you've been subjected to such an abominable crime. Scaring elderly ladies is not something we at the force take kindly to.'

Edna recoiled at the word 'elderly' but repressed the urge to say anything. She could see that the man meant well, even if he was ill-informed as to the Webster's Dictionary entry on the word. She was most definitely not geriatric, senile, or over the hill, to name but a few of the definitions. However, she was thankful for how patiently and gently he explained to her what they were going to do.

'We're going to make some modifications to your phone and install a trace, something the perpetrators won't be expecting. All you have to do is press 9 when you hear any of their voices. Please make sure to establish it is one of the parties in the investigation and not a salesman or something. Then use whatever means to keep that caller on for five minutes so that we have time to trace the call. To reiterate, once the installation is completed, all you have to do when you receive the next call is to press the number 9, which will transfer the call to a special control room, and we'll take over from there.'

'Yes, yes, I can assure you that I am in complete command of my senses, and I know what to do,' Edna said slightly acidly.

'Of course you do, Mrs Watson.' But he still reiterated that all she had to do was press 9 if she received another call and to keep the caller talking for at least five minutes.

She offered them a cup of tea, which was gratefully accepted.

'These traces are really successful,' the officer said, 'and I'm sure we'll identify the perpetrator and, of course, be prosecuting once we have proof.'

'Thanks so much, officers. I feel reassured and happy that there's something that can be done.' Edna was on a high now, and positively gushing.

'Well, everything's in place, so we'll leave you in peace and be in touch.'

Feeling reassured that she was now hopefully going to be safe, Edna went into the kitchen, made herself a nice hot cup of tea, and helped herself to two bourbon biscuits. She hoped that her little treat would take her mind off the most unpleasant scene that was unfolding with Edward Clitheroe and that the police were going to catch the people that were scaring her, thus ending this nightmare that she was living through. Then, trying to distract herself, she sat down to resume reading Iris's journal. There was a very large gap since her entry of June 1975, which Edna could only speculate about. With no one left to ask, she had no way now of knowing what did or did not happen in the intervening years. Sadly, she presumed that they were just filled with lonely days, with no events of any distinction to record.

⌀

5ᵗʰ May 1984

My friend Kate wants to introduce me to her husband's work colleague, a man called Albert, who was widowed three years ago and is looking for companionship. I have been on my own for too long now and I don't want to die a lonely woman. Reluctantly I have agreed to meet this man. No one will ever replace Bill, but that doesn't mean I can't do better than the unhappy life that I shared with Richard and the past solitary years. I still can't believe Bill gave up without a fight because I truly thought that our love was indestructible, but I was wrong. He took me at my word and no doubt found someone less complicated than me, and I have no one but myself to blame. What I do know is I will never be truly happy again. It's only now, looking back, that I can see that the night Bill and I broke up was the biggest mistake of my life and the defining incident that changed it forever.

At this point in the story, Edna could only imagine how lonely Iris had been, longing for company and the warmth of a man's arms. She now understood why her mother had agreed to meet the horrid man and how desperate she was to make it work.

10ᵗʰ *May 1984*

I met Albert in a little Italian trattoria in Old Compton Street. First impression, he was nicely dressed in a navy suit with old-school tie and polished shoes. He seemed charming enough and we talked about films we had enjoyed, but his enthusiasm for bowls and cricket left me a little cold. In general, it was a nice evening and we made arrangements to meet again on the following Thursday night. In the beginning, although it was not love, and certainly nothing like I had experienced with Bill, I felt that there was enough to enable me to settle for companionship. Edna and Don don't like him at all and don't even try to hide their dislike of him. They just say that they feel there is something unsavoury about him, although, when I press them, they tell me that they can't quite put their finger on what it is that makes them so uncomfortable. It irritates me and I have told them that if they cannot give me anything concrete, I just don't want to hear their negative comments.

✍

With heavy heart Edna was now remembering their infrequent meetings with Albert. There were sparks and unpleasant looks if Iris said anything that Alfred didn't like, and eventually she and Don decided to speak to Iris again.

'Mother, you know that Don and I are really concerned that Albert is not right for you. For a start he just doesn't seem kind to you, and we don't like the way that he looks at you. You know that we are here for you and that you can tell us anything.'

'No, he's a good man and he's going to look after me, and I don't want to be dependent upon you,' Iris protested. Eventually she got so angry with what she saw as their interference that she forbade them to bring it up again. After a few months, Iris announced that they were getting married, and Edna, not wanting to lose her mother, decided that she had no alternative but to attend the wedding and pretend that she supported the marriage.

'Look, Don, she isn't going to listen, and I spent enough time without her being present in my life when she was ill. I'm going to apologise and pretend that we realise we were wrong.'

To the end of Edna's days, she bitterly regretted taking that stance; but what was done was done, and all she could do was be there for her mother.

Soon after the wedding, alarm bells started going off. Edna and Don were not welcome in Iris and Albert's home and each time Iris visited them, Edna noticed little tell-tale signs, such as the fact that there were always ladders in her stockings. Then there were grubby marks on her clothes and then, horrifically, the unexplained bruises.

'I'm getting really clumsy,' Iris declared when questioned. 'Albert says that I must be more careful.'

Eventually, Don could stay silent no longer.

'Edna, I think that he is abusing her. I'm going to ask her straight.'

'No, Don, you can't,' said Edna nervously, which was so uncharacteristic for her. 'If we're wrong, she will never forgive us.'

'How can you even think that we're wrong?' he said angrily. 'The woman always has unexplained bruises. She clearly doesn't have enough money to replace worn stockings. Look, your mother, who was always immaculate, clearly doesn't have enough money for cleaning bills judging by the stains on her clothes. She never has anything new to wear, and the other day I asked her if she could change a five-pound note for me and she had no money. Not even enough for the bus fare home. She said that she'd forgotten to take any out, but she had her purse! I'm telling you, Edna, we have to act.'

They waited for Iris's next visit and then Don took the plunge. He gently took her hand and bravely spoke to her.

'Iris, Edna and I are extremely worried about you, and you have to know that it is safe to talk to us. We would never put you in harm's way and we will always protect you. Please, love, tell us what is going on.'

Iris started to protest and then it all became too much for her and she dissolved into a heap. It was far worse than they had feared.

'He took the money from the sale of my home, which he said he was going to put into a joint bank account and the money would become ours. I was OK with that because we were living in his home, after all. When I asked him about the paperwork, after I'd transferred the money to him, he became very violent and told me that I had no right to question him. He smacked me round the face and told me there was plenty more where that came from if I were ever to question him again.' Iris was sobbing uncontrollably.

On and on she went, as the horrific details unfolded.

'He takes me to the post office every week and gets me to draw out my pension and hand it over to him. I don't have any money of my own, not even enough to buy a new pair of stockings. Each day he hands me five pounds to go and buy provisions and I have to show him the receipt. I usually have to walk home as there isn't enough left for my bus fare.'

At this, Iris put her head in her hands and started to wail, the way she had when she and Bill had split up.

'How could I have been so stupid? Everything's gone. I have nothing, and worse, I'm so alone.'

'You're not alone! You have us and you always will. We just have to get you out of there.'

'No, no,' she screamed. 'You don't understand. He'll kill me if I try to go. I'm supposed to be shopping for supper now.'

'Listen, Iris, this is what we're going to do. I'm going to drive you to the shops and you're going to buy the food as if nothing is different. When does he next go out?'

The poor woman was sobbing into her handkerchief and trying to stave off hysteria.

'He goes to play bowls tomorrow morning at ten o'clock for just an hour.'

'Right. I'm going to collect you at ten-thirty. You have half an hour to put together a few things and then you're going to stay with us until I can find you somewhere to live.'

'But what about my furniture, photos, books, clothes? Everything that I've built up over the years?'

'Listen to me, Iris. You have to forget about all of that. Just pack a small bag with your photos and personal items, and Edna and I will buy everything you need if we can't get your things back. The most important thing is to get you out of that house. You're coming here to live with us whilst we get things sorted.'

❧

Reading her mother's account of life with the dreadful Albert, Edna was shocked to realise that she and her mother had both experienced a life-defining incident, one that changed the course of their lives. Edna, the prude, was shocked even further that her mother had been involved in not one, but two, liaisons and remembered when, a few years after Don's death, she herself had been offered the chance to meet someone described as a 'very nice man' called Lou. He was also a widower and looking for companionship.

'I don't want anyone else in my life. Don was irreplaceable and I wouldn't even want to try. Anyway, there is no way I could associate with someone who is named after a sanitary appliance,' said Edna rudely.

However, despite her protestations and somewhat surprisingly, Olivia and Viola did persuade Edna to meet the poor unsuspecting man, 'just for companionship'. To say that it did not end well is a gross understatement.

'Medallion Man', as Edna called him, turned up resplendent with a gleaming shiny gold medallion, lying against a sparse, but what was probably once luxuriant, hairy chest. He was dressed in a blue velvet jacket and white jeans, all eighty-one years of him. Edna tried to hide her dissatisfaction at her first impression and allowed him to draw her seat out, whereupon she sat down resignedly. That was Lou's one and only victory that night.

Somehow, they managed to work their way through the meal, making banal and irritating conversation.

'So, tell me about your wife. What was her name?'

'Oh, I used to call her sodding June.' Totally oblivious to the sight of Edna's arched and disapproving eyebrows, he went on, 'I called her that because she was always spoiling my fun and telling me to behave.'

Edna almost choked on her martini. She did her best to plough through the meal and after what seemed like an aeon, it was, at last, time to order pudding. Lou scanned the menu with beady eyes and, licking his lips, announced that he was having a tart.

'Well, show me the man who doesn't love a tart,' he guffawed.

That was the final straw. Edna claimed a dreadful headache and asked the waiter to call her a cab. Wanting to get away as soon as possible and not wanting Lou to leave and spoil the obvious pleasure of having his tart, she placed thirty pounds on the table, thanked him very much, and that was that.

Throughout the journey home, Edna berated herself for agreeing to go on a blind date in the first place. *When I think of my Don… This man is not worth a grain of the man that Don was.* Once was enough for Edna; she never went on a date again. But sadly, she knew that her mother hadn't got off so easily.

❧

Remembering such a horrid time, Edna was feeling that it was enough for today, and anyway, her stomach was talking to her again. Closing the book she moved to the kitchen, and spoke to Don, as was her wont at most mealtimes. Even after all the years, she still missed him terribly and talked to him incessantly.

'*I do believe that I could manage a hamburger with a nice slice of cheddar.* What about you? Shall I make hamburgers tonight? Chips or mash?' Yet again there was no response, fuelling Edna's overwhelming feelings of loneliness. She poked around in the freezer and, at last, found the ready-made burger that she had bought from the meat counter at Aldi. Humming away, she set about grilling the meat, sliced the bun and popped it into the toaster. After cutting a thick slice of cheese and placing it to melt on top, she assembled her treat and sat down to tuck in.

Edna then cleared up, which was a lot of work but, on reflection, worth it for such a nice supper. Exhausted from the calls and yesterday's meeting with Mr Roberts, Edna abandoned the book, made herself a cup of tea and sat down to watch James Martin. 'Ooh, Don, he's nearly as lovely as you,' she chuckled, and settled down to enjoy his rendition of rhubarb crumble cake with ginger cream.

No sooner was she comfortable, or as comfortable as anyone could be given her lumpy sofa, the telephone rang again, its annoying shrill setting her teeth on edge. Reluctantly, Edna rose and made her way into the hall.

'4742.'

'Allo Edna, remember me?' It was Benny the Brick.

Edna could feel her heart thumping, and not for the first time this week, she was glad that she was on her heart pills. She was trying to steady her hand as she pressed 9, thankful that, as had been explained to her, it was a silent operation, rendering the caller totally unaware of what was actually happening.

'Of course I remember you, how could I forget?' Now Edna was getting cheeky with a new-found confidence and was quite enjoying the excitement and intrigue. 'You're going to have to do better than this if you really want to spook me!' Edna was doing a sterling job of keeping the menacing Benny the Brick on the phone.

Feeling ever more confident, she was just about to tell him that she knew about their scheme to get planning permission on her house, when common sense took over and she decided to keep that up her sleeve. Instead, with a further burst of confidence, she continued talking, hoping that back at police headquarters the alarm had gone off and the duty staff had sprung into action, busily tracing the call, with a very high chance of finding him.

'Now listen, you, if you don't behave yourself, you're gonna be very, very sorry.' Edna was pleased to hear that the vulgar man sounded agitated.

'Oh no, you're mistaken. I think it's you that is going to be sorry.'

'Blimey, she really is a ballsy bitch,' she heard him say to someone.

Edna knew that she only had to keep him on the line for five minutes, but, enjoying herself immensely, she was actually reluctant to put the phone down.

'Now, if you'll excuse me, I have someone here with some urgent papers to sign.' She could hardly contain the giggle she was fighting to suppress and disconnected the call

Edna decided to call the police to fill them in, but before she could do so, the phone rang again, and this time, she was trembling.

'Hi, Mother. How are things?'

'Yes, fine.' *Why shouldn't they be? I need to calm down or their suspicions will be aroused even further, and then they'll be even more irritating than they are now.*

'Well, no reason, it's just that you've seemed more agitated than usual, and Vee and I were wondering if you've decided to go to the funeral, and maybe it would be better if you didn't go after all.' *Just as I suspected. They are pressuring me even more.*

'Olivia, I've managed to look after myself pretty well for the last seventy-odd years, and I don't need my daughters to tell me what to do.'

'No offence, Ma, we're just concerned about you.'

'Thank you for your concern, but I am perfectly fine and if you'll excuse me, I have a very important call to make.'

'I know, but…'

'What is the matter with you? How many times must I tell you that I haven't yet decided, and I don't see why the question of my attendance at that horrid man's funeral is so important to you, anyway.'

'OK, OK, subject closed. The real reason for my call was that Vee and I were wondering if you'd like to go out for dinner tomorrow night. We could pick you up. It's not much out of our way.'

Edna decided that the only way to shut her up was to accept.

'Oh, thank you, dinner would be nice, yes, lovely, but I'll meet you there.' Always needing to be in control, she just couldn't help herself; she did so like to be in the proverbial driving seat!

Having what they needed, Officer Croft now had to hand over to DCI Chief Inspector Barry Davies. However, Davies instructed Croft to remain part of the investigation, as it was his team that had traced the call, which they established was made from a telephone box in Brixton, South London. Croft was very excited to be going with the legendary Barry Davies to pick up Benny.

'So, Benny boy, haven't seen you for a long time. Exactly what do you think you're up to? You've sunk pretty low to be scaring old ladies.'

Benny just scowled at him.

'We're arresting you on suspicion of illegal activities. I must caution you that you do not have to say anything, but it may harm your defence if you do not mention when questioned something which you later rely on in court. Anything you do say may be used in evidence.'

They pushed him into a Black Maria, and down at the station, they cautioned him again, reminding him that he had the right to legal representation.

'I'm DCI Chief Inspector Barry Davies. This is Officer Croft. The time is twelve-twenty -five.' Davies proceeded to caution Benny again.

'Why did you call Edna Watson?'

'No comment.'

'We've established that you don't know her, so who paid you to call her?'

'No comment.'

'Did you use threatening language?'

'No comment.'

Benny was not being co-operative at all. Then, a breakthrough.

'OK, Benny, you're looking at three to five for aiding and abetting. If you co-operate, we'll charge you with a lesser offence.'

Benny shot a look at his solicitor, who nodded at him.

'Reg Hopkins,' he said grudgingly.

'And exactly why did Reg Hopkins pay you to do that?'

'Something about her house was holding up a big development.'

Suddenly, everything fell into place for Davies.

'Take him back to the cell.'

'Wait a minute. You said that if I co-operated…'

'All in good time, Benny. All in good time.'

Then DCI Davies turned to Officer Croft.

'Go and pick up this Reg Hopkins and bring him in for questioning. Be careful what you say. We don't want to prejudice the case in any way.'

Reg Hopkins was sitting at his desk looking at the afternoon fixtures when Mary, the little receptionist, came in and announced that the police had arrived.

'Reginald Hopkins, we are arresting you on suspicion of illegal activities. You do not have to say anything, but it may harm your defence if you do not mention when questioned something which you later rely on in court. Anything you do say may be used in evidence.'

Now, Reg was not a seasoned criminal and did not understand the rules of 'no comment'. Officer Croft could see that he was crying and shaking and knew that it wasn't going to take long.

'So, what's your interest in Edna Watson?' Davies demanded of Reg

'I, I, I wanted to buy her house,' Reg stammered pathetically.

'Oh, was it on the market, then?'

'No, but I thought…'

'You thought you would bully her into selling. Is that it? Did you cook this up all on your own? Was anyone else involved?'

'Yes. My land director, Edward Clitheroe. It was his idea. He met with her. He arranged everything. I told him not to.' His voice trailed off.

'So why does Benny the Brick say that he took instructions from you?'

Reg crumbled onto the desk.

'Take him away.'

'Croft. Go and pick up Edward Clitheroe.'

The police would never have known about Franklyn's involvement, but once faced with prison sentences, both Hopkins and Clitheroe were only too willing to tell the police about Franklyn and his obsession with Margaret. The proverbial net was closing, and the three men appeared in the magistrate's court the following day, where they were bound over pending the date of the court hearing. They were required to hand over their passports and the future was looking anything but rosy for them.

Officer Croft came to tell Edna that her ordeal was over, but she would be required to give evidence in court, the prospect of which she found very scary and exciting, all at the same time.

When the euphoria had ended, Edna was angry that she had spent so much time dealing with those wretched men, so she just grabbed a bowl of bran flakes for speed and returned to her book.

1ˢᵗ August 1994

I want to document my early childhood so that when you finally read this, Edna, it might help you to understand some of my failings and insecurities, and why I wasn't the best mother. As far as love is concerned, no mother could love more, but in terms of dependability and stability, sadly I feel that I am all too lacking.

During World War II, I was an evacuee, and my first memory was standing at Waterloo Station with a brown cardboard tag around my neck, squeezing my mother Edith's hand so tightly in the hope that she wouldn't be able to let go when the time came. Always concerned with everyone, sometimes to the detriment of her own family, my mother made a beeline for a child who was crying alone. Much to my intense sadness, what she failed to see was that instead of spending what should have been her last few precious minutes with me, she spent them comforting the lone boy, and leaving me crying alone, bereft and longing for my mother, desperately wanting her to be with me. My father, a kind man but weak, tried to make jolly conversation with me, but I was totally preoccupied with watching for my mother. Who knew when I would see her again? She just didn't realise that in her need to comfort the boy, her actions had made me the lone child instead of the boy! The train arrived and, absolutely terrified at the prospect of what was to come, I was hustled onto the train. Sobbing, I watched my mother wave as the train pulled out of the station. The journey was long and unsettling and I, together with a little boy whom I didn't know, was met by Mr and Mrs Everton. They had cold, unfriendly eyes and somehow, I knew this would not be a happy time.

One of the worst things they did was try to force me to eat what I didn't like. They could make me sit at the table for as long as they insisted, sometimes hours on end, but I would not eat tripe and onions. The mere look of it sent invitations to the bile lurking within me. I was also expected to make the beds, clear away at mealtimes, and perform most household chores, such as peeling the potatoes, cleaning the old tin bath, washing, ironing, and a host of other unreasonable tasks for an eight-year-old child. Similarly, David (the boy) was responsible for disposing of the rubbish, bringing the coal in from the coal store in the backyard, building the fire, carrying the shopping and helping me with the remaining chores. With whatever time was left to us after our long days of work, David and I devised games to play together. We made holes in conkers and threaded each with a length of string that we found in the kitchen so we could have knockout competitions. We played I Spy and the shopping list game and pretended that I was a secret agent helping the English government and David was one of Hitler's henchmen. After the war, I learned that there were some offers of a home made by unscrupulous people who were actually looking for cheap labour. David and I had been unlucky enough to have been placed with such a family, but I managed to smuggle a letter to my parents and the authorities were alerted.

I wanted to go home, but my parents refused, saying it was still too unsafe in London, so I was then relocated with another family, but this time, a very loving one. It was the first time in my tender years that I felt truly safe and nurtured. My temporary mother and father, Mr and Mrs Wetherby, encouraged me to call them Aunty Bunty and Uncle Charlie. Aunty Bunty was as soft as she was round, and always smelled of Yardley's English Lavender. Uncle Charlie was much smaller than her and very gentle. I never heard him raise his voice and he had the cutest laugh, almost like a baby gurgling. At bath times, Aunty Bunty used to wrap me up in a big fluffy towel, cuddle me and sing gentle songs like Vera Lynn's 'You'll Never Know'. Having been unable to have children of their own, Aunty Bunty and Uncle Charlie absolutely adored looking after me, a child born to irresponsible parents who were loving but unbelievably selfish and quite happy to be free to continue their life dancing the night away until the early hours of the morning. My temporary parents used to take me to the seaside for walks along the beach, where the occasional toffee apple was my favourite treat, although a vanilla ice cream cornet came a close second. When it was finally deemed safe for me to return to London, I sobbed and sobbed, not wanting to leave the only place where I had found such happiness. I was devastated at the thought of returning to lonely London and kept pleading with them *not to make me go. It was just as hard for them because I was the only daughter they were ever likely to have. I finally returned to London and went back to my solitary life. A life where my parents continued to go out dancing during the Blitz, leaving me, a terrified girl, cowering under the dining table. To add to my unhappiness and insecurity, my father, your maternal grandfather John, was a complete failure at business and we were always moving homes. He was a complete dreamer and always investing in 'sure things'. When he was gainfully employed, we had a beautiful home, and when he was out of work, he rented a one-bedroom flat with no room for me. They sent me to boarding school, and when I had to return during holiday time, I slept on a sofa. Not a way for a child to grow up feeling cherished and wanted.*

Then at the age of fifteen, I met your father, Richard, who completely bowled me over. I had the most enormous crush on him, but he quite rightly considered me too young for him. I didn't know then, but he too was besotted with me and waited patiently for my sixteenth birthday. Much to the consternation of our parents, we were married on my eighteenth birthday, which was of course far too young for me to know what I wanted.

The early days were wonderful. We were madly in love, but unbeknownst to me your father was gambling and the rest, you know.

※

It was a very abrupt ending to the entry and, as Edna read, she could almost feel the anger burning between the lines. Anger that was directed not just at Richard but at Iris's parents too, for turning her into the scared and timid woman she had become. Edna understood so much more now. Maybe more than she actually wanted to. A sudden realisation dawned on her. She knew what she must do if she wanted to have any closure on her mother's wretchedness. The wretchedness that Richard brought about, but that she, Edna, had unwittingly abetted.

So, again, she sat at her desk and googled Bill. There were many photos of Bill at charity events, polo matches and, most importantly, his obituary. There she found the name of the company he had founded, and in another entry, she found that his son, Andrew, was now at the helm. Carefully she copied the address of the company and, with an unsteady hand, put pen to paper.

⁓

PRIVATE AND CONFIDENTIAL

30th March 2023

Dear Andrew,

My name is Edna Watson and Iris Wilson was my late mother. I can almost feel your anger and your impulse to throw this letter away, but please, I beg of you, read it through before so doing.

Like your father, my mother committed suicide, completely heartbroken in the belief that the love of her life had deserted her.

I have just visited my father, who is in the late stages of Alzheimer's, and whilst there, I found a pile of letters all bound with the postmark New York. Letters that my mother never read. Distressingly, if she had not been denied access to them, I am sure that you and I would have had a most different outcome to our lives. Most disturbing of all is the letter that you wrote to my mother after your father's death. I totally understand your anger and your need to punish my mother for what you believed were her actions, but I feel it so important for you and me to know the truth about our parents. A truth that illustrates what wonderful and caring people they both were. A couple so in love that they could not bear to live without each other and yet would not desert their respective families.

I cannot imagine the pain that you have suffered, believing that your father was treated so badly, but, if you would be willing, I would love to visit New York and show you my mother's journal. A book so rich with entries full of love for your dear father. A book that would hopefully draw a line under your anger and distress.

If I don't hear from you, I will understand, but I hope you can find it in your heart to try to erase the hurt and rejoice in the happy times that they did share together. I also want you to know that, from what I have read, your father always had your mother's best interests at heart.

With warm regards,

Edna Watson

Satisfied that she had done everything possible to try and mitigate the terrible damage that had been done and feeling particularly despondent, she set about making herself a roast beef and horseradish sandwich. She felt no better after eating it and, shrugging her shoulders, moved into the sitting room, turned on the TV and promptly fell asleep. As usual, her dream was particularly disturbed and violent. She was standing behind the door, hearing the whispering. She didn't mean to eavesdrop but couldn't help it. *Muffle muffle* 'not yet' *muffle muffle* 'don't' *muffle muffle* 'best to wait until we know.' She was feeling such a sense of foreboding. She was screaming and kicking, but the gargoyles were too strong for her.

The telephone rang, waking Edna with a start. She tensed as she picked up the receiver, but it was Dr Frome.

'Afternoon, Edna, I've just had the results back and you are indeed starved of hormones. As we discussed, there is some controversy over whether it is wise to use HRT after breast cancer, but

I am of the opinion that the damage that you are doing to yourself with the symptoms is far greater than the minimal risk of a reoccurrence. Given your age, I would go ahead and restart the HRT but, of course, it's up to you. Perhaps you would like to talk it over with your daughters. Let me know what you decide, but in any event, I will check your bloods in three months' time. I think you should get the prescription filled this morning so you have it to hand, then wait until you have had a chance to fully digest the implications with your daughters.'

So excited that she might start feeling better, Edna couldn't wait for morning to come so that she could set off for the village chemist and start her HRT patches and took herself off to bed.

CHAPTER TEN

Thursday

EDNA WOKE EARLY, still anxious about the funeral. She was almost convinced that she was going to go.

I'll call Mr Timms and book him. I can always cancel if I can't go through with it. Edna was still in utter turmoil over the prospect of facing the past.

After her go-to breakfast of sourdough toast and lashings of butter and jam, she went upstairs to bath and dress. This morning, she was reluctant to leave her much-loved therapeutic and calming bath but having stayed in the tub for far too long, Edna could see that her skin had grown quite wrinkly, and she shivered as she reached for the scratchy bath towel.

She dried herself, chose a nice fleecy tracksuit to help warm her, went back downstairs, made herself a cup of tea, and rushed down to the village to get her prescription filled. She entered, proudly proffering the prescription to the pharmacist. She could hardly wait to get home to put one of the patches on. Back at the house, she ripped the package and started to read the side effects and stopped. *OK, so my head might fall off! So what? I can't carry on like this anymore.* She then proceeded to slap a patch on her left buttock.

With a busy day ahead of her, she still wanted time to read some more. She made another cup of tea, took it into the sitting room and settled down, opening her mother's book again. This was the real day of revelations; Edna was ill-prepared for the fact that she was about to pass the point of no return.

❧

1st November 1994

My dearest daughter Edna,

There is something that has dogged me since you came into our lives, and the guilt just corrodes my very being with the passing years. My darling girl, one day you are going to read this, and I beg you please to try to forgive me and not to judge, nor to be angry with me. I know that I am asking so much, but try to understand how much we have always loved you and the joy that you have brought into your father's and my life.

Try as we could, your father and I finally had to accept the truth that we were unable to have children. We were devastated and nothing and no one could console us. After two years of bitter disappointment, I asked your father to consider adoption, as I was so desperate for us to have a child. Someone upon whom we could lavish all the unrequited love that we felt. At first, he was adamant that he wouldn't, couldn't love someone else's child, but as time went on, I worked on him, and he began to warm to the idea. He and I were happy in those days, and he would have done anything to please me. Of course, it was something that he wanted too; he was just nervous that he couldn't love another man's child.

We needn't have worried. You were everything that we wanted and more.

We were told that your mother was a young girl who had become pregnant by her mother's employer. He had forced himself upon her, and when confronted by your birth grandmother with the ugly truth, he had insisted that the pregnancy be aborted. He gave your mother a thousand pounds to keep quiet and have the pregnancy terminated. Your grandmother took the money, but she had absolutely no intention of letting your mother go through with the termination. She took her on an 'extended holiday' to 'stay with friends in Devon' and set about making enquiries and arrangements to find a good family willing to adopt you. That family was your father and me, and we have loved and cherished you ever since the morning you were placed in our arms.

After a mountain of forms and numerous meetings and interviews, we were finally accepted as suitable parents to raise you. As the day approached, I could hardly sleep with excitement, but finally the day arrived, and your father and I made our way to meet you, our darling baby girl. We had spent weeks filling your nursery with clothes, toys, bunny rabbits, mobiles, milk bottles, teats, nappies, a cot, a nursing chair and just about anything and everything that we could think of to make your room a happy and safe haven for you. On the appointed day, we made our way to the office where the handover was to take place. I walked into the room, and I thought that I was going to pass out. My legs gave way, and your father had to steady me. There you were, the most beautiful thing we had ever seen. They placed you in my arms. You looked up at me with your beautiful brown eyes, and it was instant and reciprocal love. You have to understand, my precious girl, in those days many adoptive parents like us kept such arrangements a secret, absolutely petrified of the truth getting out, as they believed that they would lose the love of the child that they saw as their own. I knew that it was wrong to withhold such crucial information from you and I shall feel the burden of my guilt to my dying day, but still, I cannot bring myself to tell you. How do I start the conversation? How can I be brave enough to tell you that which I should have told you all those years ago? Forgive me, but I am a coward, and I just can't do it.

And so, with my admission to you, my story ends here as this is to be my last entry. I am so tired, and I just don't want to go on anymore. Yet again I am being selfish, putting my needs before yours, but I have completed my task. You are happily married to Don, you have your two adorable little girls and, therefore, my job to see you happy is done.

I love you more than words can say, but clearly not enough to go on living this miserable life.

Be happy. You are so much stronger than me and you really don't need me anymore. I was fast becoming the child and you the mother, and frankly, my darling, that's not the mother I want to be.

I have made such a mess of my life. Even the thought of breaking your heart is not enough to stop me. I have been storing my tablets and now I have enough to end this nightmare that I am living through. Edna, when you read this, as with the other revelations that I know you will find painful, I beg of you to try to understand and forgive a weak woman who nonetheless loves you very much. You have been the one light in my life, and I am just so sorry that I have let you down so badly.

With all my love always,

Mummy

Now it all made sense. This revelation was beyond anything that Edna had expected to learn from the journal, and she was horrified at the realisation that her whole life had been a lie. That her 'parents' had withheld this awful truth from her, leaving the burning question of who her real parents were. Edna, realising that not only this letter but the entire journal was directed at her, was very distressed. It was the most hurtful and devastating thing she had ever read. Before this confession she had thought that anything else she read could not upset her more than the recognition of Iris and Bill's unrequited love, but how wrong she was. Her life had changed irrevocably, and in that metamorphic moment, Edna acknowledged that things could never be the same again. Like it or not, there was no going back.

She sat staring at the open book, quite unable to take it all in. Learning about her true heritage, she just couldn't understand how Iris and Richard could have kept this from her.

Because Iris had never revealed the truth about her birth mother and the man who had impregnated her, with her gone and Richard lost in the haze that is called dementia, there was no one left to ask. She didn't have a name. She didn't even have a birth date to trace. Of course there was her aunt, but she certainly wouldn't ask her. Edna reasoned that even if she did, she couldn't trust the answer. None of this revelation changed the love that she had for Iris and Richard. Edna recognised that she had heard many stories of adoptive parents in the 1940s and 50s who never wanted their children to know that they were not born to them, frightened that telling them the truth would start a journey of confusion and disappointment whilst they searched for their real parents. Even in her shock and confusion, Edna understood their reasoning.

However, the revelation was unsettling, to say the least. To find that your whole life has been a lie and that you are not the person you believed yourself to be, having never questioned your heritage (why would you?), was deeply disturbing. To think that her mother had concealed an entire family and lifestyle from her was staggering. She wondered if she had any brothers or sisters but was sure that Iris would have revealed this in her journal. Of course, it was possible that her birth mother had married and started a family, and that Iris may not have even known of the existence of any siblings.

As she sat there stunned and overwhelmed, completely unable to take any of it in, it didn't escape her thoughts that when the doctors had asked her if there was any history of cancer in her family and she had quickly and confidently answered no, the truth was that she had absolutely no idea. She had no history whatsoever, let alone medical. It was as if she had come out of nowhere. Why hadn't Iris left any documents? She could only assume that her mother was scared that Edna might uncover the truth during her lifetime.

She desperately wanted to do some research to see if she could find out anything; but how could she, with no trail to follow? She was so disheartened wondering what had happened to her birth mother and whether she had any more children after Edna's adoption. But there was nowhere to start. It was possible her mother had subsequently married and had a family born in wedlock. Edna sat crying at her computer in sheer frustration at the hopelessness of it all. Then it slowly dawned on her that if her cancer was inherited, her mother might not even be alive. One thing was for sure, she had absolutely no interest in finding the man whose seed had made her life viable.

Then she quite spontaneously moved to the bureau, took out a piece of paper and began to write a letter that she knew would never be read, but none the less she was compelled to put pen to paper.

My dearest mother,

At such a young and tender age, did you know that you were never going to see me again? Did you know that the people unto whom you entrusted my life would look after me? Did you know where I was going? I have so many questions. Questions that sadly may never be answered.

I totally understand the predicament that you found yourself in, but the shock that I was born to another woman compels me to want to write to you, my birth mother. I tell you the discovery that you are my mother is simply beyond anything I could have envisioned.

As impossible as it is, a little part of me clings to the hope that you are still alive, and I will be able to find you. I will know you straight away because you will be a heart-stopping beautiful lady, your hair swept up in a chignon with a little hat set at a slightly jaunty angle, perched upon it. You will be sipping tea and laughing in a soft and gentle way. You will take me in your arms and hug me as if to never let me go.

I imagine each stage, at what would have been a milestone in your life and see the mother that you should have been. The proud mother standing at the school gates, the gentle mother teaching me about being a woman, the exuberant mother telling everyone about my school grades, the emotional mother when I got engaged, the radiant mother on my wedding day, the complete mother at the birth of my first child, the supportive mother when I was diagnosed with breast cancer and the thankful mother that I survived.

I don't blame you; I applaud you for the strength it must have taken to hand me over. You must have been so sad and frightened. One thing is for sure, I don't know how you were able to be so unselfish. I look at my children, your beautiful grandchildren, and doubt that I could ever be so selfless and brave. You could not have been sure that through that selflessness, I would receive a wonderful life, my precious mother, but I am living testimony that your bravery and altruism were rewarded.

I want you to know that I have had a good life, and I was always loved and cared for. My 'mother' and 'father' named me Edna and gave me nothing but love and devotion. Not being able to have their own child, they lavished endless affection upon me, and I have had a very privileged life. I tell you this not to make you jealous, but to reassure you that the gift that you gave my 'parents' was not wasted.

With all my love always,

Your daughter,

Edna

⤳

Edna was drained after drafting her letter. It was incredible that a woman capable of being so brittle and acerbic had the capacity for such compassion.

Having written her most poignant words, Edna closed her eyes, wanting to visualise her adored mother Iris, and twinkling and dazzling in her mind's eye was a little faux silver and mother of pearl heart inscribed 'Mother'. As a child, Edna had saved her pocket money diligently, wanting to buy Iris a very special Mother's Day gift. A week before the big day, with the coins jangling in her pocket, Edna ran excitedly along the street until she reached the familiar sign of Woolworths. She stood anxiously, having got there ten minutes before opening time and, after what seemed like hours, they finally opened the doors. There before her was an array of counters with deep trays full of tempting 'jewels'. Her heart was beating so fast, she could hardly catch her breath for excitement, thinking of the joy that would beam from her mother's pretty face when she opened her surprise. It was all so tempting, but there, jumping out at Edna, was a locket about two centimetres long and as light as a feather, proudly hanging from a very fine faux silver chain. Handing over her hard-saved pennies quickly, Edna ran all the way home to hide the gift. A gift that was to become Iris's most treasured possession.

Feeling overwhelmed by emotion at the memory, Edna went upstairs and removed the locket from the stand and stroked it carefully, wanting to feel close to her mother, the only mother that she had ever known and who had suffered such a turbulently charged life. After all, although she realised that her natural mother had given birth to her, Iris was her mother, and nothing would ever change that. Edna would be eternally grateful to her parents for giving her a home and love: who knew where she might have ended up, if not for them?

Feeling absolutely exhausted and with a late night ahead, Edna decided to have a short nap. She lay down on the sofa and within moments she was dreaming that she was being frogmarched into a courtroom with Edward Clitheroe. Just as the judge placed the black cap on his head the buzzer on Edna's alarm startled her, alerting her to get ready for dinner with the girls. Shaking and perspiring profusely, she went downstairs and into the kitchen. She moved to the fridge and peered in.

'What do you fancy tonight, Don? Oh, wait a minute, the girls have asked me out for dinner. It's just you, so I'll leave you to take out whatever you fancy.'

Then she went upstairs and laid out the black shift that she had once bought from Valeria Rossi's Mode Fashion. Mr Timms was collecting her at seven o'clock, leaving plenty of time to meet the girls at a quarter-past-seven. Edna undressed and then out came her electric Carmen rollers. She had bought them in the 1970s, preserving them carefully. They still worked as well as ever, probably because she rarely used them, but today they were a necessity. Then came the hardly ever worn makeup, and after ten minutes basic application of a pinch of Yardley natural rose rouge cream, a dusting with Revlon translucent cream puff powder, a touch of Boots No7 blue eyeshadow, a light brush of her Max Factor mascara wand, and finally applying her favourite Revlon Cherries in the Snow lipstick, she looked quite respectable. There was even a glimmer of what had once been a very fine young woman.

She was really ready for a celebratory drink and maybe she might just tell the girls about her ordeal, now that it was nearly over.

Edna, Olivia and Viola met up in the foyer of La Maison and were shown to their table, which was gleaming with its polished silver and sparkling glasses. The napkins were so stiff, you could have wrapped a gift in them. Coming towards them was a tall, thin man, a sickly smile on his face. He pulled out Edna's chair and placed the napkin on her lap with a great flourish. Olivia and Viola seated themselves.

'Bonsoir, Mesdames. Could I offer you some water? Steel or sparkleeng?'

'Water is for gardens,' Edna retorted. 'I will have a vodka martini straight up with a twist.'

Olivia and Viola exchanged glances that suggested they were resigning themselves to the fact that this was going to be a stormy night.

'Alors. Desole, Mesdames. I 'ave to tell you zat ce soir we 'ave no tete du cochon,' said the little man. Olivia and Viola stifled a giggle and whispered conspiratorially that this obnoxious little man probably came from the Old Kent Road, and the nearest he had ever been to France was a packet of Bonne Maman madeleines from Sainsbury's.

Edna, having no time for this man, announced, 'I'll have the lamb chops.'

'Mais, madame, we don't 'ave any.'

Edna rolled her eyes. 'What do you mean?'

'Lamb chops are not on our menu,' said the man sniffily. He now had a look of utter determination, as if he wished these people to be fed and dispatched as quickly as possible. It was clear that Edna was not his usual clientele at all.

'Well, everyone has lamb chops on their menu,' said Edna indignantly.

'Well, I am afraid zat we don't.'

Edna, at her most difficult, snarled, 'So what chops do you have?'

Viola coaxed Edna into ordering the duck and they settled down to enjoy their aperitif.

'Mmm.' Olivia purred like a cat having seen an unattended bowl of cream sitting two tables away. Edna could see that her daughter was positively drooling over her next target!

'All that money and good looks too.' Her eyes were sparkling like the newly polished diamond she was already imagining sitting upon the slim, elegant third finger of her left hand. Her voice betrayed that edge of excitement. The kind a person must feel whilst waiting for the last number in the lottery. She would never be described as beautiful, but she had that fascinating, slightly exotic look that made one want to stare for just a moment too long. Judging from the excitement in her whole demeanour, Edna could almost see Olivia's body trembling at the thought of bagging her latest target.

'Calm down, Ollie, he's going out with Susie Davis,' Viola snapped at her. Edna was half amused and half shocked at her daughter's revelation of her blatant aspiration to hook a wealthy man.

'Haven't you ever heard that it ain't over until the fat lady sings?'

Olivia giggled into her martini and then laughed so uncontrollably that she spilt some down her beautiful olive-green dress. It was a deliciously lustrous silk, artfully draped around her shoulders, complemented by a beautiful gold choker set with coloured stones encircling her swanlike neck, so carefully chosen to enhance her dress.

'I heard that he works out at the So Alive gym. It's invitation only, but I am sure that Jenny would put my name forward.'

'You'll have to calm down before you ask her. She would never be part of your crazy plot.'

Edna could see that Viola was clearly uncomfortable with the conversation and the discovery of who her sister really was. Needless to say, Edna was even more shocked to see her spoilt daughter, totally oblivious to their opinions, dabbing at her dress, clearly making it worse, whilst scowling petulantly at her sister.

'If you want to spend the rest of your life going to work and shopping in Zara, you go ahead, but I have more lofty ambitions for my future, which do not include saving up for our annual blowout, whilst my ex takes his new wife to The River Café for Sunday lunches. That used to be my life, and I'm going to have it again!'

Turning back to Edna, the girls tried unsuccessfully to discuss their mother's hatred toward her aunt and uncle. Playing with her bread roll, Viola started the conversation.

'So, Mother, why have you never been close to Aunt Betty and Uncle Harold? I just don't understand why you dislike them so.'

'Yes, Mother,' Olivia joined in. 'If we knew why, we could better understand and help you.' Edna felt her body contract.

'What have I always told you about privacy? I have always respected yours. How many more times must I tell you that I don't want to know when you are kissing, and I don't want to know when you are making up, and I would like you to afford me the same courtesy. So, for the very last time, I want to make it clear that the subject is closed.' And that was that.

Edna was struggling to hold it together, but all she could think about was the letter. The letter that had shattered her to the very core. She was trying to concentrate on the girls' chatter, but all she could think was: *Your mother was born out of wedlock. Illegitimate! You don't even know who your grandparents were! I am hiding a shameful secret that affects you, and some unscrupulous men are trying to swindle me out of my house.* The thoughts were going round and round in Edna's head, and she just didn't want to eat. She badly wanted to go home.

The starters arrived and the foie gras that Edna had been dreaming about was just played with and discarded. When the waiter cleared away, his obvious disgust that these rich people could order the most expensive thing on the menu and just discard it like a bottle of milk that had turned sour did not go unnoticed. The duck, although delicious, was abandoned too, and Edna didn't even want to order a pudding, which was a first. The meal that was supposed to cheer her had quite the opposite effect, and all she wanted was to get back to the comfort of her bed, where she could cuddle Don's pillow and try to forget.

All the way home, a very agitated Edna pondered the day ahead and wondered whether she would be able to go through with her plan. The evening had been a disaster and, on reflection, going out and trying to forget what had the potential to be such a turning point in her life was unrealistic. And that was before she had found out about her heritage.

Once home, she decided to call it a night and hobbled up to bed. Her back was really giving her gyp tonight, and so, much as she really wanted her 'midnight snack', especially after only picking at her supper, Edna just couldn't muster the energy to go down and fetch it.

She undressed, laying her clothes on the bedroom chair because she was just too tired to hang them up, went into the bathroom, opened her jar of Ponds cold cream and removed her makeup carefully. This was an added task that was not usually necessary as she hardly ever wore makeup these days. Irritated, she continued with the job, brushed her teeth and got into bed. She turned out the light and then struggled to go to sleep because the girls had dragged the whole wretched affair back on to centre stage.

I know that they meant well, but why oh why can't they let things be? They think that it's something to be sorted and made better. It can never be made better. Maybe tomorrow will give me some sort of closure, but it can NEVER be made better. It was like one of those children's toys when I was little. Once the tin was opened and the snake jumped out, try as I could, I never managed to get the lid back on again. That was especially true tonight, as she thought about her parentage.

She turned on her bedside lamp, and as an extra aid, she popped one of her 'calming down' pills, turned out the light, and within minutes, she was asleep.

Tossing restlessly and yet again feeling that she was on fire, Edna tried to reassure herself. *Tomorrow I will start to feel better, I'm sure. He did say after seven days I should notice an improvement...* and finally, she fell asleep.

Waking with a start, shaking and trembling, Edna was on fire again. She got out of bed, went into the bathroom, stood in the bath and doused herself with cold water. She dried herself, chose another nightie and gingerly made her way back into the bedroom. She really didn't know which was worse - the dreams or the raging fire in her body that would not abate. *When are those blasted patches going to start working?*

CHAPTER ELEVEN

Friday

EDNA WOKE EARLY and went downstairs. She took two croissants out of the little freezer compartment on top of her fridge. Licking her lips, she took out the Danish Lurpak unsalted butter and a pot of Wilkinson's strawberry jam. A mug of hot sweet tea later, Edna was feeling brighter. It was amazing how her mother's devastating admission and the prospect of what lay ahead today still had not diminished her appetite.

The sun was streaming in through the sad and neglected house, heralding the start of this important day. It was, in fact, perhaps the most important in her sixty seven years. Feeling thirsty, Edna rose, picked up her plate and mug, placed the plate in the sink to be washed later (no dishwasher for Edna), and made herself another mug of tea. She set it down on the table and tried to calm herself.

She checked her watch and made her way upstairs to bathe and dress. Whilst the water was running, she laid out her only suitably funereal garment, an A-line dress that thankfully covered a multitude of sins. Remembering the last time she had worn it, on what was undoubtedly the worst day of her life, she acknowledged that the day on which she had lost Don, the love of her life, was even worse than the day at the zoo.

Today was a day of remembrance, and again she asked herself where she had gone wrong. How could she have known at the age of five that she had, in fact, done nothing to warrant her aunt and uncle's behaviour and the trauma that followed?

On and on Edna went, vacillating about confronting her aunt. No, she decided, as she stepped into her bra and panties; it's too late to challenge my uncle, but that terrible woman must pay. She sat on the bed and rolled up her silk stockings (reserved for special occasions), pulling them up to her thighs and attaching them to ancient peach-coloured suspenders, which she doubted most young girls would understand at all. Don had understood them very well and had loved undoing them whilst slowly rolling the silk down her beautifully formed legs, over her once-slim calves and down to her dainty ankles. All at once, the memory both saddened and comforted her. Wiping a tear away, she moved to the dressing table yet again to apply her rarely-worn makeup.

Even remembering how irritating it was to have to remove her makeup last night, she conceded that she really couldn't attend the funeral without it. She rubbed some Nivea face cream into her skin and then repeated her beauty regime from the day before, finishing with a thin coat of her sparingly worn lipstick. Hating change in any form, she was annoyed by the way her favourite makeup brands got discontinued far too often, and she absolutely refused to stand in a shopping centre in full view of everyone and have some overly made-up young girl with eyelashes like a giraffe tell her that some very expensive product with a ridiculous name would suit her. She moved into the bedroom, unzipped the black dress, and stepped into it. She tamed her wild hair with some hand cream (a trick she had learned in one of those Sunday supplements), perched her black hat on top of her head, stepped into her sensible black court shoes, placed her handbag on her arm Maggie Thatcher style and, with one last look in the mirror, made her way downstairs to wait for Mr Timms.

Placing her bag on a kitchen chair, she opened the freezer.

'I'm going to be late tonight, love. You know I've got that funeral. I'm taking out a steak and kidney pie which will be defrosted when I get back. Won't take long to heat up.' Again, the deafening silence, reminding her that Don was gone, never to return to her.

'Just time for one more cup of tea,' she muttered, and again sat deep in thought.

Turning her attention back to the funeral, she wondered whether she would actually have the courage to go through with it. Would she really confront her aunt, or would she creep away defeated and ashamed that she didn't have the guts to follow through?

'*If you don't take the opportunity to deal with it, then I don't want to hear any more of your moaning,*' her alter ego's voice was admonishing her.

The doorbell rang and a startled Edna collected her thoughts and made her way to the front door. After checking that she had her keys, she locked the door and walked to the car, trying to ignore the palpitations pounding unforgivingly in her chest. If the doctor had not checked her out when she had bluffed her way into the appointment last week, she would have been convinced that she was about to join Don. *Would that be a bad thing?* On the one hand, she would love to think that she and Don could meet again and continue their marriage in whatever form that would be allowed up there. On the other hand, she was terrified of death because she had this fixation that Don, her parents, past friends and acquaintances would all be there sitting in judgment on her, whilst she stood there full of shame for her bad thoughts and sometimes unpleasant behaviour over the years. *No, best to carry on for as long as possible,* she decided.

Mr Timms held the door open for her and she settled back in the seat.

'Open the window, would you? It's dreadfully hot in here. I'm about to expire.'

Mr Timms dutifully did as he was commanded.

Winter didn't bother Edna at all. Since the return of the horrendous heat that roared through her body like an Australian bushfire, there was not actually a season that left her feeling totally comfortable.

She dozed fitfully throughout the journey, going right back to the beginning, experiencing flashbacks so real they transported her back in time to a most frightful place, one that never failed to make her feel wretched. She was told that she had not been a difficult or surly toddler, in fact, quite the opposite; but then that 'incident' had happened…

'Where's your money, Edna?' her uncle sniggered. 'If you don't have any money, you can't come in.'

She stood outside the turnstile, watching the grownups standing on the other side laughing. Her aunt was holding her cousin Felicity's hand tightly, whilst Edna looked on bewildered, frightened and confused. She hadn't seen her cousin give them any money, so why was she out and Felicity in? Of course, years later she realised that it had all been an attempt at humour in the worst possible taste, and certainly not a prank to play on an innocent child of five. She could still feel the terror of being left alone, or what felt like alone, longingly watching them on the other side of the turnstile and the pain of biting her lower lip to stop herself from crying. She never understood why, instinctively, she knew not to cry, but even at that tender age, she knew that it would increase their pleasure if she did.

And then she ran.

Darting through the bushes, under the trees, her strong little legs defied probability and literally flew across the grass, and all the while she was vowing to make them pay for being so cruel to her. She wanted to get as far away as possible, and she didn't want them to find her. Her chest was burning, her legs were aching, her eyes smarting.

Keep going, Edna. Run as fast as you can. Don't let them find you. Give them a fright. Make them pay.

Then she stopped, transfixed. Just next to the Open-Air Theatre, a man was standing with a funny thing peeping out from his trousers. What was he doing? She didn't want to stare, but she couldn't help herself.

'Wot you looking at, girlie? Want a closer look? Here, you can feel it, if you like.'

Edna was terrified. Never having had a brother and her father being a most private person, she had never seen a man's penis before, but whatever it was, she knew this was something that should not be happening and she was really scared. She now regretted being so impetuous and wished she were back at the turnstile with her uncle and aunt, even if they were beastly and horrid. The man started to move toward her. She tried to scream, but her mouth was so dry, nothing would come out. Instinctively, seeing her open her mouth, the man put his hand firmly over it.

'Now be a good girl and be quiet. If you don't scream, I won't hurt you. You don't want to make me angry with you, now do you?'

Her legs were as heavy as if cement had been poured into them. Within moments he had pushed her onto the ground, his hot, putrid breath making her feel as if she were going to pass out. She tried in vain to get him off her, but of course it was impossible. He was unbuttoning her coat, and she didn't know what he was trying to do to her but for sure she knew it was not going to be nice. There is no way to describe what five-year-old Edna was feeling at that moment; terror, horror, and fear not being strong enough adjectives. She was fighting to stay awake, but she was not in control of herself. At her age she could not possibly understand the pre-syncope that was occurring.

✍

Whilst she lay there struggling, Edna couldn't have known that once Harold had raised the alarm, a massive search had been instigated and help was on the way.

Thankfully, before Edna had time to think about what to do next, the police had surrounded them and led the vagrant away. She remembered Betty trying to comfort her, but Edna would not let her come near. Now she had found her voice and was screaming as loudly as her five-year-old lungs would allow: 'Get off me. Go away. I hate you. Don't come near me.'

The car rolled over a speed bump and Edna stirred. As she lay back again, she remembered that a kind lady, a female police officer, had cradled her, speaking to her in soft soothing terms which slowly won her confidence. Finally, Edna allowed the police to drive her home to her distraught parents, who had been alerted to the incident by a confession from Harold, followed by a visit from a community officer. Iris and Richard literally fell on Edna when she stepped out of the Black Maria. She remembered that she couldn't control her body. She was absolutely rigid and non-communicative, and she realised years later that they were at a total loss as to how to respond. The police were busy trying to set up an incident report, but Edna was still completely traumatised and could not, would not, tell them anything. Harold and Betty were still trying to fuss over her, but she was having none of it. Even at such a young age, as far as Edna was concerned, from that dreadful day, Harold and Betty's fate was sealed.

Iris tried to get Edna to eat something, but she merely stared at it.

'Come on, darling. I've made you your favourite cheese and tomato sauce sandwiches.' The traumatised child merely stared ahead. She watched her mother sitting patiently, waiting for some sort of response.

Edna allowed herself to be led to the bathroom and soaped in a bubble bath. All the while, Iris was singing gently to her 'You'll Never Know', that song from so long ago that Aunty Bunty had sung to Iris when she had been evacuated. Edna remembered Iris scooping her up out of the bath as she gently dried her in a big fluffy towel. She then chose Edna's favourite nightie, pulled the covers back and laid her in the bed. She placed Peggy beside Edna and lay cuddling her scared and frightened daughter, whilst stroking her hair and waiting for sleep to take over.

Edna had pretended to be asleep, and Iris left the room. Lying in the dark, she strained to hear the conversation coming from downstairs.

'What should we do? Should we take her to the doctor?'

'Let's just give it a couple of days before making any decisions.'

Edna remembered shaking, tears pouring down her face, not really understanding what had happened. She screamed out, and Iris and Richard ran back to her room.

'It's alright, darling. You're just having a bad dream. Mummy and Daddy are here. Do you want to tell me about your dream, darling?' Edna just stared at her.

Edna could never understand why no one ever referred to the incident again. Because the vagrant had thankfully not managed to do anything physical, his crime merely being to terrorise her, their overriding desire was for her not to have to give evidence, and so all charges were dropped. She never realised that they had decided that the sooner they could get Edna to forget the unfortunate incident the better. What they couldn't know was that Edna would never forget, nor ever forgive.

There followed months of disturbed nights with terrifying nightmares. It was always the same scenario, with Edna convinced that the 'bogeyman' was coming back to get her. Eventually the night-mares disappeared, and to all intents and purposes the incident was forgotten. However, it was always there, lurking in the background, and decades later, after the girls were born and Don suspected that things were not right, he arranged for her to see a therapist. After a few sessions, during which Edna admitted what had happened, the therapist said that it was not unusual for a traumatic incident to impose a lifetime sentence for a child of her disposition, five being such an impressionable age. Edna was highly irritated by the man and could not see the point in continuing. Discussing it with Don, she announced, 'Look, it happened. I wish that it hadn't, but it did. How is talking about it going to help? All it serves to do is make me think about it more, which leads me to being angrier and unhappier. No, Don, I am not going back. My mind is made up.'

Edna stirred again. The car had stopped, and she shook her head as if to throw off the memory, turning her thoughts to the impending confrontation. Then she hesitated. *Betty is ninety-six. Isn't it time to let sleeping dogs lie?* This internal struggle had gone on for years. Wanting to make them pay for what they had done to her and yet scared at the possible consequences, some of which she may not even have considered. *No. I am going to get it off my chest. I have had to live with it for more than sixty years. So what if she suffers for a few?* She exited the car with her head held high, took a deep breath and entered the chapel.

She was so focused on the confrontation that she didn't see Olivia and Viola waiting for her and, not wanting to draw attention to herself, she took her place in the third row. Felicity turned around and gave her a polite smile. Edna smiled back weakly, her heart banging so loudly she hardly heard the eulogy. On and on they went, telling the congregation what a wonderful man Uncle Harold was. Then she heard one man whisper to the man on his right, 'I can't believe how many people have turned up.'

The other one sniggered. 'That's because they want to make sure that he really is dead.'

That was all Edna needed to hear to convince her that she was about to do the right thing.

After the service, they all moved into the hall for refreshments. Edna saw Olivia and Viola making their way over to her. She was well aware that when she finally popped her clogs, her daughters would inherit a tidy sum. Being so frugal with her money, the financial stakes were pretty high, and so she smiled unkindly to herself when they rushed over, flanking her on either side. It was a most unfair and unjustified assumption.

'Hello, Mother,' Viola said, hugging her mother gently. 'Here, I've got you a nice hot cup of tea.'

Also trying to calm her mother, Ollie was nervously offering Edna her favourite custard creams and bourbon biscuits, which she accepted greedily. *Well*, she rationalised, it *would be rude to refuse.* After licking the last crumb from her lips, Edna dusted off those that had escaped onto her dress. *OK, Edna, this is your moment. If you're going to do it, do it now.* The enormity of the task that she was about to embark upon weighed heavily upon her, as if a sack of potatoes were pinning her chest down. Edna knew that she would never get this opportunity again, and so with great resolve, she searched the room for sight of her aunt. She espied her sitting alone, and wondering how the woman would respond, Edna bravely seized the opportunity. She charged as fast as her arthritic legs would allow towards the tiny, frail lady with bony shoulders peeping out from her austere dress. Aunt Betty looked grotesque with her white powdered face set against startlingly crimson cupid bow lips and scarily thin arched eyebrows, pencilled in with a surgeon's precision. Edna leaned in, about to mutter the obligatory

'Sorry for your loss' as a prelude to her diatribe, when the woman looked up into Edna's steely eyes.

'Edna, how kind of you to come. You know that Uncle Harold was sad that you spent so little time with us. We could never understand why you never wanted to be part of our family.'

'Never understand! Are you seriously telling me you don't understand why I wanted nothing to do with you? You ruined my life. Don't you know that?'

'But I don't understand. How did I ruin your life?'

'Don't you dare pretend that you don't remember.'

'Remember what? I told you I don't know what you're talking about.'

Edna could see that Betty was feeling the effect of the venom she was directing at her, and that she was trying to move away. She also sensed that the woman really didn't know what she was talking about. Edna wondered how something so enormous that it had dogged her whole life was so insignificant to her aunt that she had completely erased it from her mind.

Totally unnoticed, because all the guests were deep in conversation, Betty moved through the French doors and into the garden. Edna rushed after the terrified woman, who was trying desperately to scurry away. Eventually, because her aunt was not able to run very quickly, Edna, hobbling as fast as she could, managed to catch up with her, and without taking a breath, she blurted it out.

'I want you to be in no doubt about how much pain and suffering you have caused me. Together with your husband, your actions have dogged me all my life. You left me insecure and frightened and no amount of therapy, together with the love and support from my darling Don, has ever been able to wipe out what you did. What were you thinking to leave an innocent, vulnerable five-year-old standing on the other side of the turnstile, whilst you were all laughing at me? What pleasure could you possibly have derived from that, which caused me to lose my carefree childhood? You are a terrible woman and it's time you took responsibility for what you did.'

All the hurt that Edna had carried with her over the years exploded into her aunt's wizened and startled face, like salad cream shaken without the top screwed on properly.

Edna could see that slowly it had dawned on Betty, as the woman remembered that day. The day that she assumed Betty had pushed to the back of her mind, all those years ago, never to be visited again, until now. Her aunt was visibly distressed.

'It was only meant to be a harmless joke. I never meant to hurt you, and we couldn't have known that you would run away. I would do anything to change the events of that day, and I'm stunned to realise that you are still affected by it. Please. Edna, I'm so sorry. Please let's start again. With Harold now gone, I need my family around me.'

It all came flooding back to Betty. She and Harold had screamed for help whilst trying to navigate the turnstile exit. Many parents waiting to enter the zoo rushed forward, offering help. A member of staff, upon hearing the commotion and after questioning Harold, rang the police and gave as much information as possible.

'Five years old. Pink and white party dress, dark brown hair and eyes,' the shocked woman had responded to the call handler's questions. Then she turned to Harold.

'What's her name?'

'Edna.' Betty remembered that he could hardly bring himself to say her name. As if by saying it he would make this nightmare real. By that time, Betty was sobbing and blabbering and of no use to anyone.

'Oh, do stop it, woman,' he had shouted at her. 'We have to find Edna. Now, pull yourself together.' He was so angry with her. *The whole thing had been her stupid idea. What was she thinking?* At that precise moment, she and Harold would have given their life savings to turn the clock back.

Felicity, not understanding what was going on, started to cry and announced that she wanted to leave NOW! With no time to lose, they had grabbed the frightened child whilst they paced up and down, not knowing where to start.

Two Black Marias then pulled up outside the zoo, braking so severely it seemed they were going to burst their tyres. The officers all jumped out and descended upon Harold and Betty. They were firing questions at them, one after the other, and Betty thought she was going to pass out.

'How long ago did this happen? In which direction did she run? Why did she run? What kind of child is she? Can you confirm her name? Does she have a pet name? What was she wearing? Describe her hair colour and eyes.' The questions were coming at them like a shower of bullets. Harold was scared, but he was also frustrated that he had already given most of this information when they called the police. An officer explained that it was imperative to find a missing child within the first forty-eight hours and that as each hour passed, the likelihood that a missing person will be found decreases, making those first hours of an investigation the most critical. After that, the officer explained grimly, the chances of finding them unharmed and alive were relatively slim. Therefore, he went on, they needed to spend a few minutes collating all the details that could help them to find Edna. Harold was digesting this information and realising that it could all end in complete disaster. Betty had never been a religious woman, but at that point she was praying with all her might and desperately hoping that G-d would forgive her for her complete stupidity. The police then broke up into groups and, together with the volunteers, started searching. In all, the process took minutes, but to Harold and Betty, it seemed like hours before they were out there looking for their niece. Harold had the most unenviable task of ringing Richard and

Iris. The police had told Harold that it was imperative that Richard and Iris stayed at home in case Edna found her way back.

Betty remembered watching Harold sweating profusely. 'Hi, Rich. Listen, Edna has a bit of a tummy ache and wants to go home. Just wanted to check that you're there. We'll be back in about twenty minutes.' Harold had never before lied to his brother, but he could hardly say, *Hi Richard, Edna has gone missing because we played a stupid trick on her. Can you come?* It was decided that someone Edna knew should remain at the scene of the crime, and so Harold went, shoulders down around his knees, to tell his brother and sister-in-law what had happened, and Betty was forced to stay so that there was someone familiar when/if they found Edna.

Suddenly, there was a breakthrough. 'OK, Sarge, I think I've spotted her,' an enthusiastic officer said into his walkie-talkie. 'She's on the ground with what looks like a vagrant holding her down.'

'Don't startle him,' came the reply from his superior. 'We need to surround him, catch him unawares, and attack simultaneously. Wait for my command.'

Meanwhile back at the house Edna's father screamed at his brother, 'What were you thinking? There's no knowing what could've happened to her. I'll never forgive either of you for this.' Richard was sick with thinking of what might have happened to Edna.

Both Betty and Harold were so relieved when the officer assured Richard that, as Edna's underclothes had not been disturbed, they were quite confident that the vagrant had not interfered with her in any way. Richard wanted to believe them, but there was still that nagging doubt that would not let go. Full of remorse, Harold and Betty tried to explain that they had only meant it for a harmless bit of fun.

'Scaring a small child is not funny,' Richard replied, 'and I'll thank you for saving your jokes for your own child.'

Then Iris interjected. She was carrying Edna in from the kitchen and, in a quiet but very firm voice, scolded them, 'Oh, for goodness' sake, can we please just concentrate on Edna? I'm taking her upstairs for a bath.'

⁓

Now, after Edna's outburst, with memories flooding back at her, Betty was wailing.

'Shut up, you terrible woman! It's your own fault if you're lonely. I want no part in your life!' Edna was spitting venom at the petrified woman.

'I am so sorry. If I could take it away, I would.' Then Betty's voice dropped away, and, without warning, the woman went bright red, and her eyes looked as if they were going to bulge out of her head. Edna looked on, shocked, as her aunt keeled over and dropped to the ground with a most grotesque expression on her face. Edna screamed for help, and upon hearing the commotion, Viola and Olivia rushed over to check on their mother. They saw their aunt lying motionless on the floor and called for someone to ring for an ambulance. Felicity's cousin Tom, the local GP, was summoned, and he applied CPR, but it was to no avail. The woman was already dead.

'Oh, Mother, what a ghastly thing to happen. Are you OK?' Viola gave her visibly shaken mother a chair.

Edna had gone deathly white, and for one dreadful moment, Viola thought that her mother had suffered a stroke because she seemed unable to communicate, but Tom, after checking, assured her that it was just shock.

'Quick, Ollie, go and get her a sweet cup of tea.'

Felicity came running over and wanted to know what had happened. Amazingly everyone was so busy chatting to old friends that no one at all had seen the incident in the garden.

'Oh my Lord, how did it happen?' Felicity was devastated. To lose her father was extremely painful, but the fact that she had now lost her mother as well within a few days of his departure was too much for her, and she started crying uncontrollably. 'I just don't understand. Edna, You seem to have been the last person to see her. What happened?' By now Felicity's screaming was well out of control, and Tom was trying unsuccessfully to get her to swallow a Valium.

'I... I... I don't know,' said Edna shakily. 'We were talking about the past and then she suddenly collapsed. I don't think I can add anything else except to say that I am so sorry for your loss. Shocking, just shocking.' Edna turned away, ashamed and consumed with guilt. Everyone assumed that Betty had died of a broken heart, but Edna knew better.

Because it was a sudden death of a seemingly, albeit elderly, healthy woman, the ambulance crew summoned the police. There followed a round of questions as to what had occurred.

Once the colour had returned to Edna's face and she was talking coherently, the police insisted on questioning her before they could help her out to Mr Timms' car.

'What was her mood? What did you talk about? Did she seem unwell? Was she in pain?' On and on the questions were fired at Edna, and she desperately wanted to go home. Finally, when the police felt that there was nothing more that Edna could add, and Tom having reassured Olivia and Viola that their mother's funny turn was probably just due to shock, they reluctantly let Mr Timms take her home. They wanted to follow, but as usual Edna was difficult and insisted on going alone, but not without having promised to call once she was safely tucked up in bed. Edna was feeling wretched, and she wanted to be rid of her daughters with their prying questions as soon as she could. She let herself into the dark and unwelcoming house and decided to abandon supper. Due to the horrific circumstances, even the thought of the steak and kidney pie with its buttery pastry and succulent beef could not induce her to eat a morsel. She had really given it to her aunt, but was it worth it? Did she feel any better? Truth to tell, she actually felt worse. She thought that she would try to watch some TV but found herself unable to concentrate and couldn't relax.

'Listen, Don, I've had a horrible day. If you don't mind, I want to go to bed. Would that be OK?' Particularly despondent today at the lack of response, she trundled up to bed. She just wanted to blot it all out and go to sleep.

Mentally and physically exhausted, she made her way upstairs, washed and brushed her teeth and took out her well-worn copy of *Forgiving What You Can't Forget*, a self-help book she had plucked from the shelves of Sylvia's Bookshop years ago. She had tried to read it a few times and it should have provided enormous help, but she just didn't (or didn't want to) get it. After a few pages, she placed it back on the bedside table. Feeling quite debilitated from the emotionally charged events, she decided to call it a day and turned the lights out.

Tonight, Edna should have been snug and cosy in her winceyette sheets and fluffy eiderdown, but instead she shivered as she lay there, full of guilt at the realisation that her actions had very probably killed her aunt. She re-played the events of the day over and over again, like an old 78 rpm record stuck in the groove. Edna, full of contrition, finally acknowledged that she must change her ways. She couldn't re-write history and eradicate the pain and shame of the past, but she could let go and try to be a nicer person. *Seriously, though,* she mused, *can you teach an old dog new tricks? Well, just give it a go, Edna. What's to lose?*

She couldn't bring Don back, she reasoned, but she could continue her life in a way that would make him proud of her. In that cathartic moment, it was more important to her than anything that she didn't lose face in Don's eyes. She decided that if there was an afterlife, she wanted to face him, the love of her life, and hopefully see his pride at the woman she had finally become. Completely exhausted, she was asleep within moments.

Chapter Twelve

Saturday

EDNA WOKE EARLY, opened her eyes, looked across at the clock and was astounded to see that it was seven-thirty, which was much later than she normally slept. Yesterday had been so dreadful and she recognised that her body needed to make up for the lack of sleep over the last few weeks. She knew that she needed, no, *wanted*, to try to make amends for her aunt's death without accepting that she had had anything to do with it. Despite her guilt at what had happened, she remembered her mother's words all those years ago, when Edna had thought she had killed her grandmother. No, she reasoned, it wasn't her fault. Her aunt probably had a heart condition. *No, I didn't kill her,* she repeated over and over again like a mantra, and then determinedly she sat at the kitchen table to put pen to paper.

❦

Note to self:

Time to accept that Don is gone. Fine to talk to him for company, but don't mope about it. If he were here now, he would tell you to get on with life and enjoy what's left. His life was cut short through no fault of his own. Yours may as well be, for all the happiness you get from it.

Try to make amends for your aunt's death. Stop blaming your aunt and uncle for your lifetime of insecurities and fear. Time to let go and take responsibility for your own life.

Don't recoil at the image in the mirror. No amount of looking will change the ravages of time, so embrace those baggy eyes and that turkey neck, because they reflect who you are and who you have been.

Don't be rude and difficult with people. They are no less a person than you are, and it's time to realise that you get so much more out of honey than a lemon. A sour face is not an inviting face, and remember that everyone has their own problems and most hide it well. Oh, and don't be intolerant. Remember that no one is perfect, including you!

Draw a line down the page and hope that the good memories outweigh the bad and don't obsess about how much time is left. Reflect on the good stuff that has passed. Stop feeling like there is more behind than there is to look forward to. Just live in the now, enjoy and be present! Finally, acknowledge that time and friends are the two things that become more valuable the older you get.

Oh, and never wanting anyone to sit close to you on the bus is ridiculous, and that horrible habit you have (if someone dares to sit down) of looking straight ahead and with a menacing voice uttering, 'Did you bring the money?' has to stop. It never fails to amuse YOU how quickly people move, but, Edna, it is unbecoming.

Edna was feeling particularly hungry and made herself some porridge, even though it meant washing a saucepan, because she didn't hold with 'micro-ovens', as she called them. She stirred the gloop and ate it quickly, disregarding the perils of the dangerously hot mixture.

Savouring the last mouthful, she was unsure whether it was the breakfast or the list of promises she had made to herself that had done the trick, but she was feeling calmer and happier than she had since

Don had died. Of course, it wasn't the porridge. It was her admitting to her faults and her covenant to be a better person. One last thing that she added to the list was that she was also going to try to eat more healthily.

She went upstairs, drew her bath, lay back in the velvety water and closed her eyes. It suddenly occurred to her that for the last twenty-four hours, there had been no forest fire in her body. It was such a natural transition that she hadn't even noticed. All she knew was that it was brilliant, and she was so grateful to Dr Frome and to the manufacturers of those little bits of plastic that held the panacea to so many of her problems. There was a lot that was bad about living in England in the 2020s, but there was also some pretty amazing stuff, and this was definitely one of them.

With so many tasks ahead of her today, there was no time to waste, and so she stepped out of the bath, dried herself quickly, and chose the Liberty print dress normally reserved for special occasions.

The phone rang, disturbing her thoughts. She trundled downstairs to the hall and sat on the chair by the console table and lifted the receiver of her avocado-coloured rotary telephone, surely now a collector's piece. It was Olivia, making sure that she was OK.

'Morning, love,' said Edna chirpily.

Edna could almost hear her daughter choking on her Greek yoghurt and granola and stifled a giggle.

'Mother, are you OK? How are you feeling this morning?'

'Much, much better. In fact, I was thinking that it would be nice to have a family get together. I could buy some rotisserie chickens from Waitrose; you could make a salad, and maybe Viola would make her chocolate cake. What do you think?'

'Yes, Mother, that would be lovely.' Something in Olivia's voice gave away that her thoughts were elsewhere. 'When are you thinking?'

'How about Thursday?'

Olivia gulped. Was the notice too short for people? 'We'll certainly try Ma. Your birthday, of course. What a great idea.'

Edna was secretly quite chuffed that they might make a fuss of her birthday, which was totally out of court with her usual feelings on such suggestions.

'Very well, I will call Viola now and let you know what she says.'

'No, it's OK. I'll speak to Viola, and you just let us arrange it.'

'Very well. I'll wait to hear from you.' Edna was already humming.

❧

No sooner did she end the call with Edna than Olivia dialled Viola's number.

'Hi, it's Ollie, you won't believe the conversation I just had with Ma. She wants to have a family get together, and she actually agreed to a birthday celebration! She wants to have it on her birthday! We're going to have to move pretty quickly to arrange that. We'll just have to have a ring around and see who can come, or, more likely, who wants to come! You don't think she suffered some kind of episode yesterday, do you? Should we get her checked out?'

'Are you kidding? She'd never agree. Let's just keep a watchful eye over the next forty-eight hours and then decide. No point in getting her all agitated and worked up over nothing, is there?'

Reluctantly, Olivia agreed, but still… she had an overriding feeling of unease.

❧

Edna lifted the receiver again and dialled the number of Pretty Lady, the local hair and beauty salon.

'Hello, Edna Watson here. Would it be possible to make an appointment for a cut and colour on Wednesday morning, please?

188

Yes, ten o'clock would be excellent,' she replied to the voice on the other end of the line. 'I shall see you then.'

Edna disconnected the call excited at the prospect of the lunch.. *A family get together. It's been so long. Maybe I should cook the chickens instead of ordering them, and perhaps some of my new potatoes, with lots of butter and mint?* She lifted the receiver and dialled the next number.

'Good afternoon, Harding's, how may I connect your call?'

'I should like to make an appointment for a makeover at nine o'clock on Thursday morning. I want a more mature lady. Not one of those silly girls with body piercing and tattoos.' Then the new Edna bit her lip as she realised how rude she had been.

'I can assure you that all of our technicians…'

Technicians, Edna thought, *what on earth does that mean? What happened to 'beautician'?*

'…are totally professional,' the girl on the telephone continued.

Edna sighed. 'Yes, I'm sure they are.' Hastily, she made the appointment, as she had one more important call to make.

'Hello, Felicity, it's Edna. I was just wondering how you are doing.'

From the silence, Edna could almost imagine a very startled Felicity swallowing hard.

'Well, Edna, you were the last person I expected to hear from. Yes, I'm not doing too badly, under the circumstances.'

Unsure how to continue, Edna plunged in headfirst. 'So, when will your mother's funeral be?'

'We are waiting to hear about the autopsy.'

Edna nearly choked. 'Why will there be an autopsy?'

'Because my mother died under suspicious circumstances.'

'What do you mean, suspicious? She had a heart attack, she was ninety-six years old, and she had just lost her husband. What's not to understand?' Edna said, just a little too bombastically.

'I think that I would rather not talk about it.'

'Yes, yes, of course.' Edna tried to sound sympathetic under the guise of trying to be friendly, but she just needed to ask one final question.

'Didn't she have existing conditions?' Edna just needed to know whether she had actually killed her aunt.

Felicity ignored her. The conversation was completely tiresome, with both of them wondering what the hell was the point in continuing when they had absolutely nothing in common.

Edna tried again to be more sympathetic. 'Is there anything you need? Anything I can do for you? I know we have never been that close, which was mainly our grandmother's fault, but I really do want to help, you know.'

'Why was it our grandmother's fault? I don't understand.'

'Oh, Felicity. I don't want to dredge up the past. It's all water under the bridge now, but suffice to say that you were her favourite, and I always felt like a second-class citizen.'

'That's weird, because I always felt inferior to *you*. You were always so dismissive of me, and I could never understand what I had done wrong. Maybe we could now have a better relationship?'

Edna considered this, and could imagine her pathetic cousin looking wistful, and so she tried as best she could to be nice. 'Look, Felicity, we have never been close, have we? But I think that we now have a better understanding of each other, and we could try to meet up on a more regular basis. After all, we are both all that's left of the old family. Except my father, of course, but in the poor state that he's in, he doesn't really count,' Edna said sorrowfully. 'One day, I'll try and share with you the reason for my unkindness to you. It was never your fault and I know that I have treated you badly. Anyway, do let me know when the arrangements have been made and promise to call me if you need anything.'

Edna tried not to notice the disappointment in her cousin's voice as she said goodbye.

She was frustrated that Felicity had not answered her questions about her aunt's health but acknowledged that the point of the call was actually to make amends for her actions, not to assuage her guilt.

She reflected on what she had been through in her life and just what an incredible few weeks it had been. Then she turned her attention back to her party. *A get together just for me. Well I never… Now, I think it calls for a new dress. Everything in my wardrobe is so drab and dreary or well past its sell-by date. Yes, a new dress, what fun.*

For the first time in years, Edna approached the day with curiosity and anticipation instead of despair.

Finally, calls made, she decided on an early lunch and after much rustling in the freezer, out came the remembered cheese sandwich that she had frozen on a previous occasion, when she had decided that two toasted sourdough sandwiches full of oozy cheddar cheese were too much, even for her! This was perfect for a lazy day such as this. She placed it in the Breville toaster and laughed as she remembered her crude comparison with a mammogram.

Then a sadness moved over her, and she made her way into the sitting room. Once more she began talking to Don. 'I'm so looking forward to the party but it's the first thing that I have truly celebrated since you left me, and it makes me so sad that you won't be there by my side. I mean, I know that you will be here in my heart (at this she placed her hand gently but firmly upon her chest), but I long to feel you again. Really feel you. To feel your physical presence holding me, kissing me, stroking my hair and making me feel like the most loved person on this planet.' At this, a lone tear travelled down her lined face, and she clumsily wiped it away with her sleeve.

'Well, this is not going to get the baby bathed,' she exclaimed, suddenly pulling herself together. 'What about a nice cup of tea and a biscuit?' As usual the silence hurt, but she put the kettle on and delved into the biscuit barrel. "Now where do I keep the spoons?" After rummaging around in the cupboards, she found the cutlery drawer and dismissed the nagging thought; why had she forgotten where she kept them? "Let's watch Countdown she said with a false cheerfulness."

As was becoming a common occurrence, Edna couldn't concentrate on the programme and her mind wandered back to the disclosure of her adoption. 'Am I ever going to stop wondering about my birth mother? Is she still alive? Is the vile creature that impregnated her still alive? I don't know whether I can live with the uncertainty. Do I, in fact, have siblings? Do Olivia and Viola have aunts, uncles, and maybe even cousins? In not telling the girls, am I not perpetuating the lie that my grandmother instigated? Oh, Don, I wish that you could tell me what you think and what I should do.'

It was now early evening, and Edna still feeling blue and in need of comfort food, ordered a pizza. After devouring a large tomato, mozzarella, mushroom and artichoke special, she cleared up, turned off the lights and made her way upstairs.

CHAPTER THIRTEEN

Sunday

EDNA OPENED HER eyes and congratulated herself that she had slept through the night. What with the previous nightly visits to the bathroom and the raging fires, this was surely a good sign.

She made herself some toast and jam, deciding that she could have eggs for lunch when she got back from visiting Marjorie.

She entered the bathroom and turned the shower on, checking the water before she stepped in. Although she loved her therapeutic baths and repeatedly professed that she didn't enjoy showers, she had to admit that they were actually pretty therapeutic too. She submitted herself to the oncoming assault of spray; the penetrating needles pounding into her back, and she was really feeling quite invigorated as she stood under the torrent of water that threatened to invade her skin. She reached for the shampoo and gave her hair a good rub until her scalp felt slightly sore. She soaped herself well, taking care to check her breasts and ignoring the desire to leave that part of her ablutions. She knew only too well the dangers of failing to carry out checks and how lucky she was that she had regularly done so.

She stepped out of the bath and wrapped herself in one of her old scratchy towels. She noticed how scaly her legs were becoming and promised herself that she would try to remember to use moisturiser. She dressed in her 'old faithful' tracksuit and went downstairs to the hall cupboard. She selected her trainers and a gilet and made her way down the path and along the road to the village, to pick up some newspapers, a bottle of milk and a loaf of bread before her visit to Marjorie. She arrived at the house, took the key from her pocket and called out as she entered.

'Cooeee, Marjorie, it's me, Edna.' Out from the kitchen hobbled the little lady with a walking frame, obviously overjoyed to see Edna.

'Oooh, Edna, I do so love Sundays. You're an absolute treasure!' Edna chuckled to herself, thinking that of all the adjectives used to describe her, most people would not use 'treasure'.

After enjoying their Sunday cuppa, Edna bid her farewell and made her way home. It was now lunchtime, and yet again her stomach was talking to her. She made herself a cheese omelette topped with baked beans and sat at the kitchen table with the *Sunday Times* spread out to the side of her. There followed pages and pages of depressing news, and after deciding that she couldn't bear to read any more, she read the culture section full of books and TV programmes. She skimmed over the theatre pages as she never ventured into London anymore, and she certainly wasn't interested in the beauty and fashion sections. The travel section lay neglected.

She had been so obsessed with her mother's journal that she hadn't read a novel in a long time, but today she was going to start reading *The Nightingale by Kristin Hannah*. Yes, it was time to get back to normality, and on one of her rare visits to town, the lady in Daunt had told her that it was excellent.

After being engrossed in the book for about two hours, Edna wandered into the kitchen to select something for supper. She opened the freezer and her hand hovered over the lamb chops. 'Come on, Edna, spoil yourself. What's a dirty grill-pan against the pleasure of juicy lamb chops with mint sauce and redcurrant jelly?' She placed the wrapped chops in a bowl of iced water and two hours later the chops were defrosted. She couldn't remember where she had learnt this trick, but it was a lifesaver. She washed, dried and seasoned the meat and placed it under the hot grill. At the same time, she placed some new potatoes and a few leaves of mint in a saucepan and watched the chops as they started to sizzle and fill the kitchen with their wonderful aroma.

Feeling contented after such a delicious meal, Edna attacked the washing up with renewed vigour. 'How about watching Stanley tonight?' she announced to the empty room. 'At least my stomach won't be rumbling this time,' she said chuckling to herself.

After an enjoyable episode based in Calabria, with mouth-watering fall-off-the-bone lamb, she announced, 'I'm off to bed, love. It's been a lovely day, but I'm pooped.'

Chapter Fourteen

Monday

EDNA WAS FULL of anticipation as to what she might find to wear. Iris had always been an extremely elegant woman and exquisitely dressed until she no longer had the budget to indulge her shopping habit, but Edna had expressed no interest in fashion since Don had died and was quite astounded at her change of heart. She walked to the bus stop, actually noticing and enjoying the abundance of vibrant colours that adorned the window boxes lining the rows of houses, twinkling like jewels in the bright sunlight. Humming out loud, she hailed the oncoming bus. Tom, the driver, slowed to a halt and Edna stepped onboard.

'Thank you, driver. Frimlington Proper, if you would be so kind.'

Tom, whom she saw often, was clearly shocked at her cordial behaviour.

As she neared her destination she actually asked Tom if he could possibly stop the bus so that she could get off, and she was still humming when she entered Valeria Rossi's boutique. Edna surveyed the grotesque-looking woman. Thin and bony, with flamboyant over-the-top makeup, bell-bottom trousers, a ruffled shirt that would have rivalled the best pantomime dame, and costume jewellery that could have gone into competition with Mike Oldfield's Tubular Bells, Valeria launched herself at Edna.

'Ciao, Meezis Watson, Long time no sea. Ima so pleezda to see you Entrare.' Edna uncharacteristically allowed the woman to air-kiss her on both cheeks and the game began.

'Whatta can I do for you todayuh?'

'I'm looking for something for a special occasion. My daughters are hosting a get together for my birthday,' Edna said proudly.

'OK, so letta me look at you. Sizea fourteen, no?'

Edna nodded, and the woman started darting around, pulling things out, shaking her head and replacing them. After about ten minutes, she had five things trailing over her arm and she ushered Edna into a fitting room.

'I'ma notta gonna show you, because they needa to be seen onna. You know clothesa don't always have hanger appeal. Trusta me, Meezis Watson.'

'Oh, call me Edna, please!' By now, Edna was quite enjoying her new persona.

At the invitation to call her by her first name, Edna chuckled at the sight of Valeria nearly choking on the gum that she was surreptitiously chewing at the back of her mouth.

'Ova coursea. Come, Edna, let's trya these onna.'

Edna tried on the first dress, a floral shift with a short-capped sleeve to hide the bits that women of a certain age need to hide, and she had to admit that, although Valeria had no idea how to dress herself, she certainly knew a thing or two about dressing other women. Edna pulled back the curtain and allowed Valeria to survey her.

'Yessa, yessa.' She pulled the waist in a little and pinned the hem slightly shorter. 'We put it onna the sidea and trya the nexta.'

Edna then tried on a flowy silver-blue blouse with some palazzo pants. She couldn't believe how different and, yes, almost lovely she looked.

'Oh, I love this. I don't even want to try anything else. It's so glamorous and it actually makes me feel so special. This is definitely it!' she exclaimed with glee.

She watched Signora Valeria clap her hands together with joy.

'How much is it?' Edna started to ask, and then she went on, 'Actually, I don't care. I'll take it.'

Edna couldn't help noticing the sparkle in Valeria's eyes. She could only imagine that, after Valeria had told her it had been a slow start that morning, Edna had increased the woman's takings considerably by having chosen the most expensive outfit in the shop. Valeria carefully wrapped the outfit in tissue paper.

'Havva wonderful party, Edna. Anda thanksa so mucha for coming.'

It was a lovely bright day and Edna was feeling happier than she had in years. Clutching her special purchase carefully, not wanting to crease it, she made her way to the greengrocer.

'A coz lettuce, a pound of tomatoes and a cucumber please. I'm making a salad today,' said Edna proudly, whilst patting her stomach. Bert the greengrocer, who was a habitual gossip, with something to say about everyone in the village, was for once rendered completely speechless. In twenty-five years of trading in Frimlington, he had never known that terrible woman utter anything other than a rude word about his veg.

Back at home, she placed the food on the kitchen table and carried her outfit carefully up the stairs. Unwrapping the reams of tissue paper, Edna finally held up her outfit and just gazed at it for a very long time. Then reluctantly, not wanting to let go, she carefully hung it on the wardrobe door and went downstairs. She almost danced into the kitchen with her new found peace of mind. After searching for the saucepan, she hard boiled an egg and set about washing the lettuce. Determined that she would not eat anything that would spoil the way she looked in her outfit, she sliced the tomato and cucumber, peeled the egg, sprinkled some Sarsons vinegar over the top and made a conscious effort to eat slowly, chewing every morsel. She didn't enjoy it at all but it did feel good. After washing up, she moved into the sitting room and sat down to watch some TV. Edna winced, feeling the lumpy sofa as if for the first time, making a mental note to get someone to have a look at it.

'I bought myself a beautiful outfit today, love. It's for my party on Thursday. I do hope you like it.' A moment of sadness washed over her, as she thought about how much nicer it would be if Don were to accompany her. Then she gave a shiver, as if to banish the sombre mood and announced to the empty room. 'Let's watch the Northern Lights with Joanna Lumley tonight. We never did get to see them, did we, Don?'

After thoroughly enjoying the programme, Edna made her way to bed. She was exhausted after such a full day and after carrying out her nightly routine, she almost fell into bed and was fast asleep in minutes. This time there were no nightmares, in fact the following morning she didn't remember dreaming anything at all.

Chapter Fifteen

Tuesday

AFTER DEMOLISHING TWO slices of sourdough toast with black cherry jam, Edna went upstairs and drew her bath. Inhaling the familiar scent, she lay back to relax. She congratulated herself on the improvements she was making and decided that she must stick to her diet. Then she dressed quickly, took a leisurely stroll to the village and headed for the fishmonger. As she moved towards the door, she little realised that her approach was inspiring horror in the shop assistants, who knew that one of them would be unlucky enough to have to serve her.

'Oh no, Phil, look who's coming! It's definitely your turn today.'

'But I've got to gut this salmon,' Phil replied.

'It's your turn, 'cos I'm going to count the fish,' his colleague chortled, and walked to the back of the shop.

'Good morning, Phil, it's a lovely day, isn't it?'

The poor man nearly choked on the hot cross bun he was snacking on behind the till. In fact, you could probably have knocked him over with only a plaice fillet.

'Good morning, Mrs Watson. How can I help you?'

'I would like a nice piece of cod for my supper, thank you very much. I shall leave you to choose.'

Over the last forty-eight hours, unbeknownst to Edna, the mystery surrounding her behaviour had been the sole topic of conversation in the village. No one could understand the metamorphosis, but they welcomed it all the same.

Phil selected a nice slice, wrapped it up and handed it to her.

'Four twenty, please. I'm afraid the cod's a little pricey today.'

'No matter. I can't take it with me, can I?' Edna giggled. 'Here's a pound for your trouble. Bye now, and thanks ever so.'

She left Phil standing there scratching his head and wondering who this woman was and what she had done with Edna Watson!

Edna couldn't wait to get home and try her outfit on yet again. Humming once more, she smiled at strangers as she passed them. Some walked on, but a few actually smiled in return.

Back at the house, Edna turned the key, entered, and for the first time in years she saw her home as others would see it, noticing how horribly shabby everything looked. She made a mental note to find a local decorator to cheer the place up and definitely someone to repair her lumpy sofa. She went straight to the kitchen, placed the fish in the fridge and removed an apple, pear and a small piece of cheddar for her healthy lunch. She then went straight to the bedroom, reached for the outfit hanging on the wardrobe door and again tried it on. She stood looking at her reflection and really liked what she saw. She was about to re-hang her special outfit carefully, ready for her party and go downstairs to make a cup of tea, but paused to gaze at herself in the mirror for the umpteenth time. For the first time in years, Edna cared about her looks, in fact, very much so. *How could I have walked around looking like a bag lady? What must everyone have thought? What must the girls have thought?* She made herself a promise never to let herself go again. *I'm going to have a cup of tea, but I'm not going to have a biscuit. I don't want it to be too tight,* and she congratulated herself on her newly found self-discipline. Then she reluctantly removed the outfit and went downstairs for a cuppa.

The whistle went, she made her tea and then sat down at the kitchen table to make a list of all the jobs that needed attention in the house, but she just couldn't remember what they were. She struggled for a while and then remembered, jotting it down quickly lest she forget again.

'It's going to cost a pretty penny' she mused, 'but what else am I going to do with the money?

She was finally going to enjoy her beautiful home and bring it back to its former glory. *It's going to cost a pretty penny, but what else am I going to do with the money? Anyway, it will make the house more valuable after I am gone, which will no doubt please my girls,* she rationalised. *Now, now, Edna, let's stop that. So what if they inherit everything after I'm gone? It won't make any difference to me; I won't know about it, will I, or at least I hope I won't.* Edna had never feared death, just so long as that was 'the end'. No, what spooked her was the thought that she would be floating above, watching everyone and unable to communicate, and that those who had gone before, also 'up there', were standing in judgement, knowing exactly how she had behaved.

Brushing those thoughts away, she finished just in time for *Countdown* and settled down to watch. She responded in a very good-natured way when someone began struggling with the numbers.

'Oh, poor thing. You needed to multiply by the seven and then take away the three plus the five.' Unlike the old Edna, with her rude retorts, she was genuinely sympathetic to their struggle.

Feeling pretty exhausted after such an action-packed day, she nodded off and was soon dreaming that she was meeting her birth mother. As she had always imagined, her mother was sitting at a table. A most beautiful woman, very elegantly dressed, yet soft and fluid and not austere in any way. She rose and ran towards Edna.

'My beautiful daughter, I never thought I would see you again.' She took Edna in her arms. So realistic was the dream, Edna could practically feel the warmth of her mother's body.

Edna woke with a start and, after watching the *Six o' Clock News*, went to the fridge and selected the cod, some butter, a lemon, two potatoes, a hunk of cheddar, and some milk.

'Look what I'm making, Don. No Birds Eye frozen dinners for you. No, no, it's my special cod and creamy mash. Only the best for you!' She set about washing the fish, poaching it in milk and boiling the potatoes. She hummed as she creamed the potatoes and piled the mash on the cod before placing it in the oven to brown. Then she spooned the fish pie onto a plate, eyeing it hungrily, but she was now eating with her newly acquired discipline of chewing properly, placing her knife and fork back on her plate between bites and savouring each mouthful.

'Oh, that was lovely, Don. I did so enjoy it. Did you? Do you remember that I told you there was something I was going to tell you? I didn't want to worry you, love, but I have had a bit of a bother with an unscrupulous property developer. I reported it to the police and it's all over now. You should be very proud of me. I handled it just as you would have done, and guess what? The girls are making a birthday lunch for me tomorrow, and I'm really excited. Do you like my hair? I'm having a makeover tomorrow, all in aid of my special day. What a laugh. Your Edna, being done up like a Christmas Turkey!'

Tonight was different. She was not downtrodden because she had no response from him. She just took comfort in nattering to him as if he were there.

Edna didn't want to think about her mother's journal tonight. She didn't want to be sad. She just wanted to look forward to her special day and wished that her nagging doubts about her aunt's autopsy would go away. Felicity's shock announcement had really unsettled her. She went slowly upstairs and readied herself for bed. Within moments, she was asleep and dreaming that they were all at the funeral. Her aunt pushed against the lid of the coffin, jumped out, and started screaming at Edna.

'You killed me. Get the police, she's a murderer!' Two people grabbed Edna, and she was trying unsuccessfully to break free. She was crying and telling them that they didn't understand and there had been a dreadful mistake, but no one would listen, and they were dragging her into a Black Maria.

Edna woke, heart pounding, shaking and crying. She sat bolt upright, reached for her bedside table, popped one of her 'calming down' pills, and waited for the panic attack to subside. It must have taken her a full five minutes to start to calm down, and then, blissfully, a relaxed sleep took over.

CHAPTER SIXTEEN

Wednesday

EDNA WOKE EXCITEDLY with an unusual lack of appetite, and after a quick bath, walked to the village and entered the Pretty Lady Hair Salon.

'Hello, love, I'll be with you in a minute,' came the voice of a rather stout and cheery woman, probably aged about fifty. 'Come and sit here. Tea or coffee?'

'Oh yes, thank you so much, a cup of tea would be lovely.' Edna was really enjoying this new-found delight of spoiling herself and being cosseted.

After about five minutes the woman came back with a cup of tea and a tiny wrapped biscuit which Edna declined. 'Now let me look at you.' She fussed around lifting sections of Edna's hair. 'I know what we should do. Will you trust me?' Edna nodded. The woman disappeared again and returned with a bowl of very strange looking sludge and set about sectioning Edna's hair until Edna looked like a cross between a Dalek and a hedgehog. Finally, she brushed the sticky stuff all over, paying special attention to Edna's grey roots. Peering at the reflection in the mirror, Edna was fascinated.

Half an hour later, she was led to the basin where she lay back in the chair whilst the woman began pouring warm water over her head, removing the silver foil and then vigorously massaging her hair with a most delicious-smelling shampoo. She rubbed and scrubbed, and Edna had to acknowledge that she never gave her hair such a thorough wash. Next came the conditioner, and this time a more relaxing massage. All too soon the chair was raised, and Edna was placed in front of a mirror.

'Now, what would you like? It certainly needs a good reshape, if you don't mind me saying.'

The old Edna would have told her that she most certainly did mind, but today she saw the wisdom of the woman's words.

'Yes, you are quite correct. It's my birthday party tomorrow, and I want to look as good as possible. Mind you, I don't want to look like mutton dressed as lamb. You look sensible, so I'm going to leave it to you.'

The woman set about snipping and clipping and shaping. When she was satisfied with the shape and length, she placed a large blob of what looked like foam on Edna's head and then began blow drying Edna's usually unruly hair.

'What about rollers?' a slightly perturbed Edna asked.

'Oh, we don't use those anymore. You just wait and see – you'll love it.'

Edna decided to go with the flow and when her hair was done, she did indeed love it. She stared at the mirror and was ecstatic with her transformation.

'Gosh, what a difference, love. You look ten years younger.' Edna could see that the hairdresser was surveying her handiwork appreciatively.

Overwhelmed by the reflection in front of her, Edna readily agreed as she pressed five pounds into the delighted woman's hands.

Her stomach loudly reminding her that she hadn't eaten today,

Edna made her way to the coffee shop. She entered, settled herself at the table, and smiled at the waitress. The friendly young girl smiled back.

'What can I get you?' She almost sang it.

'Oh, a nice frothy cappuccino, please.' Edna salivated at the thought of that sweet foam and felt so much lighter. 'And an egg salad and ooooh one of your delicious Portuguese pasteis de nata tarts. You know, the ones with the sweet set custard in the middle.' Edna licked her lips at the thought of what was to come. To her delight, the waitress returned with the indulgent treat and Edna smiled broadly.

Having enjoyed it so much, Edna ordered another of their delicious cappuccinos and thought about ordering another tart, telling herself that they were, after all, very small, but then, totally out of character, the newly reformed Edna tapped her stomach and decided that one was enough. *There will be plenty of sweet things tomorrow, I'm sure.* She smiled her lovely smile that had not been seen not been seen in such a long time.

It was a lovely day, and Edna was really enjoying her daily walks for the first time in many years. She noticed things that had escaped her because she was now looking up and ahead, instead of studying the cracks in the pavement. 'I think I'll make myself a nice tuna salad for supper. Don't want to look bloated in my new dress.' Again uncharacteristically, Edna chuckled to herself. Today, she was definitely not falling asleep on the sofa and chancing spoiling her hairdo. *I might just sleep sitting up tonight,* she said to herself, laughing. *Ooh, Edna, you're getting really vain!* She laughed again. Edna had enjoyed such a wonderful day.

After her healthy supper, having watched an episode of *Planet Earth*, wondering at the beautiful polar bears, Edna made her way upstairs, washed, brushed her teeth and, after propping pillows against the headboard so that she didn't lie flat and spoil her hair, she fell asleep, despite her excitement at the prospect of tomorrow.

CHAPTER SEVENTEEN

Thursday

AT SIX O'CLOCK, Edna woke again full of excitement at the day ahead. The new, slightly vain Edna went into the bathroom, checked her reflection in the mirror, and was delighted to see that her hair had hardly moved. She decided on a light breakfast, as she was sure there was going to be plenty to eat and she wanted to be able to enjoy it. She had no idea that there was such a large guest list, and actually, the girls were more than a little apprehensive this morning that maybe they had gone a step too far.

She went to the pantry and pulled out the Weetabix. She placed two in a bowl and poured the ice-cold milk on top. Only one teaspoon of sugar later and she was ready to enjoy her breakfast. She scanned the headlines of the paper, but today there was just too much going on in her head for her to really concentrate. She finished her breakfast and went upstairs for a leisurely bath. After readjusting the water because she had mistaken the hot water for the cold, she laid back and relaxed. Within moments, her mind was wandering. She imagined walking into Viola's home and seeing a big banner proclaiming 'Happy Birthday!' Her children and grandchildren would all be there in their finest clothes, and she imagined everyone making such a fuss of her new look. There would be a huge cake upon the table, surrounded by chicken, potato salad, green salad, cheese and biscuits and a large fruit platter. Her stomach began to growl. She stepped out of the bath and grabbed one of her incredibly scratchy towels. *And that's another thing. I'm going to buy some new towels whilst I am at Harding's.*

Edna dressed quickly, making sure that she wore something with buttons so that she wouldn't disturb her makeup when she dressed for the party. She had spoiled herself and booked Mr Timms for the day. He drove her to Harding's and said that he would wait for her in the car park. First stop for Edna was the linen department. She fingered the fluffy towels, each one softer than the last, and then looked at the prices. *How much? That's daylight robbery! I'm not paying that!* And then she stopped. *Who am I saving it for? I'm going to start enjoying my life.* She selected two towels with matching hand towels, face cloths and bathmat, and headed for the cash point. With ten minutes to spare before her makeover, Edna made her way to the salon.

'So, what's the special occasion?' The over-enthusiastic woman started attacking Edna's face with a rather gloopy cold cream.

'My daughters are organising a lunch for my birthday,' Edna said proudly. 'Could I please ask you to be careful with my hair? I have had it restyled for the party.' In the old days, before she had possibly killed her aunt, Edna would have sniffily told the girl just to get on with the job, but today Edna was enjoying the banter. She lay back in the chair and realised how incredibly lovely it was to have someone massaging, primping and fluffing over her face with a host of differently-shaped brushes. Finally, the half-hour was over, and the woman raised the chair and invited Edna to survey her new look.

'Is that really me?' Edna could hardly believe her eyes. The transformation was incredible. 'The girls won't know me. Oh, thank you so much. I just love it.'

The woman puffed up as proud as punch and smiled joyfully when, for the second time in twenty-four hours, Edna gave a generous tip of five pounds.

Edna went out into the car park to meet Mr Timms and, as soon as he reached her house, she jumped out like a spring chicken, eager to try on her outfit yet again.

With plenty of time before dressing, Edna elected to read the travel supplements that had lain unread and neglected since last weekend. She started with the cruise section. As she flicked through the pages, she decided upon a European cruise that would take in Venice, hoping that she could recreate those wonderful days with Don. *Yes, that's what I am going to do. Can't take it with me! What an adventure that would be.*

Edna looked at her watch and judged that it was time to get ready. She was so excited at the prospect of a gathering which was just about her. *If I have time, I can always call the agent while I wait for the car.*

She went upstairs, carefully stepped into her outfit, and surveyed herself in the mirror. Gone was the haggard-looking woman who had stared back just days ago. *Was it really only a few weeks? My life has changed so dramatically since then, and the girls aren't even aware of most of it.* The woman looking back at her now was pretty and well-groomed, with smiling eyes. Her hair was lustrous, having been properly cut and swathed in conditioner for about an hour. Her makeup, courtesy of the makeup artist, was totally appropriate for a woman 'of a certain age', *but certainly not elderly!* The silvery blue silk top with the slightly darker Palazzo trousers complemented her hair perfectly. She stepped into her silver dancing shoes, which had lain unworn for too many years, and she felt… *I don't know how to describe how I feel. Joyous,* she supposed. *That's it. I feel joyous and blessed.*

⁓

Meanwhile, at Viola's house, the guests were all assembled, waiting to see Edna's reaction when she saw them all. Viola got the impression that there was great trepidation as to whether Edna would stay or turn around and leave in a huff, but she sensed a feeling of hope. The one thing Viola knew they had all agreed upon was that Edna had survived cancer and had experienced a most traumatic time at the funeral. They were all there to let bygones be bygones.

There were second cousins that Viola knew her mother had not seen for years, and everyone had brought their extended families. All in all, it was quite a crowd. Viola contentedly surveyed the scene. Everyone had brought a prepared dish with them, and the table groaned, resplendent with all the many and varied offerings. Coronation chicken, poached salmon, fried fish goujons, crudités complete with a selection of dips, Thai beef curry, meatballs, rice, potato salad, mixed salad with asparagus and avocado, beetroot watermelon and feta cheese salad. Chocolate fudge cake, apple and blackberry crumble, oranges in Marsala, and fruit salad. There was far too much food, but Viola knew that Edna was going to be tickled pink to see such a mouth-watering display. The birthday cake, a concoction of vanilla sponge and strawberries, was hidden away in the greenhouse lest Edna saw it before the allotted time.

⁓

Back at Rose Cottage, Edna went downstairs and sat at her kitchen table in her finery. She couldn't decide whether she was more excited at the prospect of her trip or the party. With some time until Mr Timms was due to arrive, she decided to call the travel agent whilst she waited for him. She dialled the number, her heart fluttering ever so slightly.

'Good morning, Silver Cruises, how can I help you?'

'Hello, I need some advice. I should like to talk to someone about a cruise to Venice.'

'If you could just wait a moment, I'll put you through to the relevant department.'

After a few seconds, another voice came onto the line.

'Good morning, how may I help you? Hello, hello, hello – is there anyone there?' *How rude,* thought the girl. *I didn't even keep her waiting five minutes.*

❦

After ringing the bell three times, Mr Timms alerted Miss Viola that he could not raise her mother. The guests were all assembled and nervously looking at their watches; the mumbles had already started:

'I knew she was difficult, but not turning up to her own party – well, that's something else!'

'Surely she wouldn't do that to the girls, after all the trouble they've been to organising this.'

'This really takes the biscuit. And to think I was beginning to feel sorry for her.'

The whispered gossip went on and on.

One hour later, Olivia and Viola let themselves in with their emergency key.

Olivia could still hear her mother's instructions as she turned the key:

'You just remember that this is my house and I want my privacy. I am only relenting and giving you a key for a strict emergency.'

Well, this was an emergency, wasn't it?

She and Viola entered the house, and everything was unnervingly quiet. Olivia checked the garden first. *Maybe that's why she hadn't heard the door.* Viola checked the bedroom and the bathroom, but Edna was nowhere to be seen.

'Cooeee, Mother, it's us just checking all is OK. Where are you?' To their very profound dismay, they entered the kitchen and found Edna, in all her regalia, beautifully coiffed hair, perfect makeup, looking more beautiful than they had seen her in years, with her head lying sideways on the kitchen table, the travel supplement spread out, and a huge smile upon her face.

Epilogue

WEEKS LATER, THE girls met at Rose Cottage to clear Edna's house and make arrangements for the inevitable sale of their family home. Having stepped over the mail, deciding to deal with it later, they made themselves each a cup of coffee and then set about the unenviable task of going through their mother's worldly goods.

'Let's make three lists,' Olivia said. 'One for charity, one for sale and one for personal possessions that we might like to share. You take upstairs and I'll start down here.'

'Ollie, look at this,' Viola exclaimed, bounding down the stairs. She handed her sister their grandmother, Iris's well-worn and treasured journal.

'This is our grandmother's record of her life. Look, and there's another that looks like a book draft. It seems that Ma was writing a book continuing the story.'

'What do you think the old girl had to say?'

'More importantly, what do you think she had to say about us?' The girls laughed conspiratorially.

'Our mother, writing a book. I never knew that she had it in her.'

'She must have been reading both of them recently because I found them by the side of the bed. Let's stop for a bit and have a look.'

They downed tools, entered the sitting room and settled down side by side on the sofa, placing the journal and the draft between them. The tears were soon rolling down their cheeks as they began to unravel their mother's most complicated life. When they realised what must have been Edna's profound shock upon learning that her mother was not her birth mother, they began to understand the difficult and unfathomable woman that was their mother. The revelation about 'the incident' with her horrifying encounter with the vagrant was beyond anything they could have imagined. Now they were learning of the threatening behaviour of the crooks that were trying to cheat their mother out of her house, the loss of the love of their grandmother's life, a man named Bill, the vitriolic letter written by his son informing Iris of Bill's suicide, the heart-breaking 'farewell' letter from Bill, the abusive and disastrous second marriage that Iris suffered, and her suicide. Then they read of the guilt that Edna suffered, thinking that she might be responsible for her aunt's death by confronting her at the funeral. It was all too distressing to take in.

'If only she had trusted us.' Viola was sobbing uncontrollably by now. 'We could have supported her better if we had been able to understand her.'

'I know,' a particularly contrite Olivia replied. 'What awful things to live with. Just one would have been difficult enough, but to have suffered so much trauma, well, it's no wonder that her heart gave out. She was so strong, I think she could have dealt with everything life had thrown at her, but not Dad's death. That's where it all went wrong for her. I think that after he went, her heart was truly broken.'

It was getting dark before they turned the last pages of their grandmother's book of revelations and their mother's unfinished draft. Totally exhausted, sad and bewildered, they went into the kitchen and raided the cupboards, looking for something that would resemble sustenance.

'This isn't going to feed the starving troops!' Viola exclaimed. 'One mouldy potato, a slice of stale bread and curdled cream isn't going to get us anywhere!'

'For someone who loved food so, I'm shocked to find this is all there is! Let's order Uber Eats and work on. I don't actually think I want to come back again. I'd rather get this over with. What do you think?'

'Agreed. Let's hit it, and we can always sleep here if it gets too late. Although I'm not sure I'm ready for that. Let's see how it goes.'

'Agreed,' they chimed in unison and then, bin liners at the ready, went back to the task in hand. Sadly, most of Edna's life went into the black charity bag, but there were a few things, like the Chanel jacket and Gucci handbag, that were saved. When they came to the silver locket, although it was obviously a worthless piece of fake jewellery, the inscription 'Mother' and the fact that it was given pride of place on their mother's dressing table told them it was really special to her. They decided to keep it and work out in whose house it should remain. As for the furniture, aside from their great-grandmother's stool, it was all unusable, and so they agreed that in the morning they would make arrangements to have everything removed.

'What about selling the house?' Viola asked her sister. 'Who shall we call? After what Ma went through, let's play it safe and call in a couple of reputable agents to compare.'

'Great idea,' said Olivia. 'We'll call in the morning.'

Each girl made her way to her old bedroom, and they kissed goodnight. Viola lay in the cold room tossing and turning but sleep just wouldn't come. She kept imagining noises and finally, desperate to get some rest, she padded into Olivia's bedroom.

'Are you still awake? Shove over. I need a cuddle.'

Olivia turned to her younger sister and put her arms around her. 'Just you and me now. We have to look after each other.'

Despite thinking they would find it difficult to sleep, they were so exhausted from the trauma of losing Edna and the shocking revelations in Iris's book, that they were dreaming within moments.

First thing the following morning, Olivia put on her most haughty voice to call the agents.

'Hello, I should like to speak to someone about our late mother's house.'

After supplying the required information, they made appointments for valuers to come and inspect the property. Then they had the unenviable task of making funeral arrangements.

'Do we know what her favourite song was?'

'Not a clue, and I'm none the wiser about her choice of poetry.'

'Well, we have to choose something.'

'Wait a moment. What about the quotes in her journal?'

Excitedly they opened their mother's draft, looking for something suitable.

'Here we go, how about this? It's short and sweet, but I think it's lovely.'

Tell me what else should I have done?
Doesn't everything die at last and too soon?
Tell me what it is you plan to do?
With your one wild and precious life?

The Summer Day by Mary Oliver

'Oh, Vee, I think that's perfect. Well done. Let's put it on the Order of Service with a nice photo. One of Ma in happier times, when Dad was still alive.'

❧

The day of the funeral came, and the girls had agreed that they would deliver the eulogy jointly. 'Let's face it, she didn't have any friends, and we're the only ones who knew the true Edna.'

That statement turned out to be totally incorrect. There were far more people than they had expected, and a lot of them were complete strangers.

Slowly, the girls realised that there was yet another side to their mother, as people came out of the woodwork to tell them what Edna had quietly done for them. There was the family that Edna visited every Harvest Festival and Christmas time with a huge basket of food, aided and abetted by Mr Timms. Another talked of her charity walk to raise money for cancer treatment for their ten-year-old child. A nurse told of Edna's baking sale at the hospital to raise money for research into heart failure The superlatives about Edna went on and on.

'Are they talking about our mother? I feel like I didn't know her at all.'

'I know, it's surreal,' Viola replied.

The vicar then called upon the two girls to stand up.

With hearts thumping and palms perspiring, they took their places at the lectern.

Viola spoke first, quickly re-adjusting her opening words.

'Hello, everyone. We would like to pay tribute to the woman that you all knew as Edna Watson and the remarkable lady that we knew as our mother. The woman who we now discover secretly worked to help others.' Viola stopped and Olivia took over.

'We are sure that to many of you our mother was a grumpy, difficult and sometimes rude woman. True, she didn't suffer fools gladly, but to those who knew her well, all the people she helped in her lifetime, it appears that she was an angel in wolf's clothing.' At this, everyone nervously giggled and cleared their throats.

'Actually, deep down she was really compassionate and kind,

but she hid behind the impenetrable facade that she had erected to protect herself.

'She was born in 1954,' Olivia continued, 'and until quite recently, she had no idea that she was adopted. Certainly, we had no idea, and we have been amazed at the story we have been reading, which is chronicled in our adopted grandmother's journal.

'Edna lost the love of her life, our father Don, just over twenty years ago, and from that day life lost its glow for her. So it appears that she threw herself into helping others less fortunate than herself. To her credit, she never told anyone, least of all us, her daughters. She just quietly went about her business, not needing any accolades or acknowledgements from anyone.'

Viola ended the tribute, saying, 'What I wouldn't give for just one more day, one more chance to tell her how much I love her, and how very proud Olivia and I are to be able to call her our mother.'

With tears streaming down their faces, the girls sat down.

People were coming up and congratulating them and enjoying the bourbons and custard creams specially served in honour of their mother.

There were those who had wonderful stories to repeat about Edna, and equally those who were as dumbfounded as the girls were when they discovered the real Edna Watson.

'Who would have believed it?' the dentist exclaimed. 'What a dark horse she was!'

'I know,' said Charlie, the fishmonger. 'Although she was acting out of character that last time she came in. Actually gave me a tip.'

One by one, people chipped in with stories about the woman whom they had judged so harshly, although to be fair to them, she didn't let them in to see what a special lady she was.

When the last people had left, Olivia and Viola hugged each other, and agreed to meet up at the house the following day.

Recognising the potential of the land, both agents delivered a very welcome surprise for the girls. It turned out that the house was extremely valuable, and both firms estimated that they might well get two million pounds. The girls were first speechless and then completely elated.

'A million each!' Viola exclaimed excitedly. 'That's life-changing, Ollie.'

Two months later, they entered the house for the last time, to empty the final contents ready for the new owners. They climbed over the pile of mail and walked into the kitchen and filled the kettle. Sitting at the table over a cup of tea, they found it so weird that Edna was not there with them, pontificating about something or other.

'If you don't want it, I should like to take that blasted whistling kettle,' Vee giggled.

'Be my guest. If it's OK with you, I've been thinking that I should like the locket. I know that it has no value, but it's particularly grounding for someone like me to recognise that jewellery does not have to be valuable to be priceless.'

'Oh, Ollie, of course you can. I can always look at it when I visit. You take it with my blessing.'

'One last thing before we leave. I think we should go through the mail, see what needs dealing with, and make a list of whom we have still to contact.'

Knowing when she was beaten by her younger sister, Olivia gave a big sigh and went into the hallway to retrieve the post. She returned and her face was ashen. Trembling, she handed Viola an envelope very clearly postmarked USA. 'Here, you open it. I can't!'

Dear Edna,

I received your letter this morning and must admit that I am very shocked. Shocked to learn the truth and shocked to be re-hashing all the terrible memories of the past. Of course, I am uncomfortable to have written such a ghastly letter to your mother, but you understand I had no idea what was really going on. That said, I don't want to rake up the past, merely to apologise for what I wrote, so I would really rather we left it here. I bear no ill will to you and your family and wish you all the best.

Yours,

Andrew

⤧

Both girls simultaneously rose and hugged each other, knowing that this was truly the end of the saga.

The following month, when all the hubbub had died down, the two sisters, now closer than they had ever been, boarded a flight for Livorno to begin their homage to Edna. They had booked a cruise that would take them to Venice, following in the footsteps of their parents at their happiest time.

They stepped out on to the balcony of their luxurious suite, courtesy of one woman's most frugal ways, and raised a glass of champagne to a most unusual yet incredible woman. Their amazing mother, Edna.

Bio

JACKI RACKE was born in London. She has had a varied and interesting career, including the release of three pop records in the 60s, before working as a model agent in the early 70s. This is her debut novel, which she started during Covid, following an initial creative writing course and subsequent Alumni mentoring programme with Curtis Brown Creative. She lives in London with her husband Laurance, where they love spending time with their four children and eight grandchildren.

ACKNOWLEDGMENTS

I give thanks to the following people, without whom I definitely would not have written this book.

Linda Blaustein, my dear friend and 'sister from another mother', who, on a weekly basis without fail, filled me with the strength and courage to keep going.

Anthony Trevelyan, an author and my mentor, for encouraging me, supporting me and pushing me to be the best that I can be.

Linda Rosenblatt, who convinced me that I was good enough to give it a go.

My many dear friends, some of whom agreed to read my very early ramblings.